HEARTS CRY:
MADE WITH PURPOSE FOR A PURPOSE

HEARTS CRY
MADE WITH PURPOSE FOR A PURPOSE

How to live in Purpose and on
Mission for God's glory

SHIRLEY
CHARLES-ROBINSON

HEART'S CRY: MADE WITH PURPOSE FOR A PURPOSE
© Copyright 2021 Shirley Charles-Robinson

All rights reserved. No part of this publication may be reproduced, distributed or transmitted in any form or by any means, including photocopying, recording, or other electronic or mechanical methods, without the prior written permission of the publisher, except in the case of brief quotations embodied in critical reviews and certain other noncommercial uses permitted by copyright law.

Although the author and publisher have made every effort to ensure that the information in this book was correct at press time, the author and publisher do not assume and hereby disclaim any liability to any party for any loss, damage, or disruption caused by errors or omissions, whether such errors or omissions result from negligence, accident, or any other cause.

Adherence to all applicable laws and regulations, including international, federal, state and local governing professional licensing, business practices, advertising, and all other aspects of doing business in the US, Canada or any other jurisdiction is the sole responsibility of the reader and consumer.

Neither the author nor the publisher assumes any responsibility or liability whatsoever on behalf of the consumer or reader of this material. Any perceived slight of any individual or organization is purely unintentional.

The resources in this book are provided for informational purposes only and should not be used to replace the specialized training and professional judgment of a health care or mental health care professional.

Neither the author nor the publisher can be held responsible for the use of the information provided within this book. Please always consult a trained professional before making any decision regarding treatment of yourself or others.

For more information, email info@shirleycharlesrobinson.com.

Soft Cover ISBN   978-1-7378999-0-7
Hardcover ISBN   978-1-7378999-1-4
EBook ISBN   978-1-7378999-2-1

ENDORSEMENT REVIEWS

Shirley's words point us to a good and loving God who 'made us on purpose for a purpose.' This book is packed with scripture and actionable steps to awaken our hearts and minds to the voice of God.

~ **Juli Boit**, Founder & International Director of Living Room International, author From Beyond the Skies

Shirley Charles-Robinson provides actionable steps to find your purpose, grab hold of your God-given identity, and get off the "hamster wheel of life" so you can pour energy into the things that bear true and long-lasting fruit. This book and the lessons within it are a powerful reminder that we all have a purpose, and our purpose is meant to be shared, expressed, and fostered. Our past, our thoughts, and our fears do not have to hinder us from living the abundant life that God desires for us.

~**Blythe Hill**, CEO/Founder Dressember Foundation

We're all on a journey to live the purpose for which we were made and Shirley Robinson is a trustworthy guide. I've known Shirley as a friend and church leader. Her guidance is grounded in Scripture and forged in the ups and downs of her own path to purposeful living. You will be encouraged and come away with a greater vision of God and his vision for you.

~**Cheryl Fletcher**, Executive Leadership Team-Discipleship for Menlo Church, Menlo Park, CA

Readers will find Hearts Cry encouraging and inspiring, rich with scripture in every section and rich with stories that paint what this journey could look like, including her own. I appreciate her openness with her own struggles as well as her personal background as a child of immigrant parents. Shirley Robinson provides many practical steps along the way to help the reader discover their unique purpose God has for their lives and, as she says, "to awaken those God whispers that lie dormant in the recesses of your mind and heart."

~**Sandy Lee Schaupp**, Spiritual Director with InterVarsity Christian Fellowship

Shirley's voice is a heartfelt guide in the wilderness, beckoning others to follow the path to life. She cultivates a space that invites reflection, healing and truth-changing freedom to sink in and transform the reader. By sharing her own life, she uses her experience and wisdom to usher us into a journey of growth, discovery and God's goodness. I felt like I was having coffee with a beloved mentor who was encouraging me to be the woman God created me to be.

~**Colie Kreuger**, Lead Pastor for Women's Ministry with Christian Assembly, Eagle Rock, CA

DEDICATION

*To my late mother Piedrecita Blanca Charles
and my late father Jean-Claude Charles
your memory lives on in me.
You both would have
found pleasure in this book.
Forever in my heart!*

*To the women whose voice and purpose
has been stolen from sexual exploitation
of all kinds or felt they had no alternatives.
May you gain your identity
and purpose back from
the One who calls you His Beloved!*

*To my kids,
Emiliana, Dewain II, Dominic,
Donavon & Kayla
may you walk in the purpose
for which you were created.
You have my heart!*

TABLE OF CONTENTS

FOREWORD	1
ACKNOWLEDGEMENTS	3
PREFACE	7
PART 1 AWAKE: ARISE TO THE CALL	12
PART II RECONSTRUCTION: PREPARING FOR THE JOURNEY	34
PART III KNOW THYSELF: YOUR EARTHLY HISTORY	62
PART IV KNOW THYSELF: YOUR SPIRITUAL HISTORY	104

PART V	120

ALL WILL BENEFIT:

BRING YOUR GIFTS TO THE ALTAR

PART VI	138

POSTURE:

WE ARE MADE TO GLORIFY HIM

PART VII	150

BATTLE READY:

PUT ON YOUR ARMOR

PART VIII	180

LACKING NOTHING:

EQUIPPED WITH ALL THAT YOU NEED

PART IX	196

PLAN:

CHART YOUR DESTINATION

PART X	228

ACCOUNTABILITY:

CHOOSE YOUR RUNNING PARTNER

PART XI	248

LEGACY:

THE REWARD OF FINISHING WELL

For a free 7 Day Devotional please visit:

www.ShirleyCharlesRobinson.com

You will also find resources
to start and lead an effective small group discussion
to discover your unique purpose in community.

FOREWORD

I have led a house of prayer in Pasadena (PIHOP) for the last fifteen years and see almost daily the desperate need for the remedies found in this book. I have enjoyed getting to know Shirley, as we have sung the Word weekly on a team in our community. She is an openhearted, deep vessel that is always ready to receive more from God.

In an age when you can manicure and project whatever image you want to portray of yourself, the need for real connection to our hearts in the safety of God's grace and truth is so needed. Shirley gives easy access to this reality. By taking us on an eighteen-inch journey, through the difficult terrain from our head to our heart, we explore new caverns hidden within, where we mine for the gold that God exquisitely etched into our being from the very beginning. When you read this book you will plow new paths into your treasure-filled identity and receive skills to live out your God-given purposes.

In your quest for authenticity and a meaning-filled life, I want to endorse Heart's Cry: Made with Purpose for Purpose. May you enjoy this simple and profound journey Shirley has paved in answering your heart's cry to becoming your true purposeful self.

Cheryl Allen
Executive Director of Pasadena International House of Prayer

ACKNOWLEDGEMENTS

The success of a person is never theirs alone or achieved alone. It is always achieved by countless individuals who may never know their contribution. Their contribution can remain unacknowledged and remain anonymous unless mentioned. It is with humble gratitude that I thank my God-Sized Goals Group: Debra Kreuter, Phoebe Kimble, Paola Smith, Diana Namara, Marva Sutton, Anjanette Harris, Diane Gohl, and Mary Makarios. You will always hold a special place in my heart. In the year 2018, among this group of amazing women, God whispered this book to me. I am forever grateful for your trust and your contribution to my development as a leader. Irene Rogers, you believed in the concept of this book and gifted me a getaway to be with God. On that weekend, God gave me the blueprint for this book. Grateful for you!

My sisters Ruby Noble and Alexandra Shim-Chim, the Charlie's Angels, I am forever grateful for God's wisdom in ordaining our forever bond. You two are my confidants, my helpers in time of need, women whom

I admire and respect greatly. I love you both! Myrlene "Myrl" Schenck, my soul-sister, we have done life together from afar. I value your authenticity, trust, and love. Karina Bonnefil, "sister," who is a fierce defender and advocate. You keep me laughing; I love you!

Sonja Warfield, my prayer partner in life. We have prayed countless mornings for years during the unexpected twists and turns of life, for the birth of this book, and for the hands it would one day occupy. Love you! My prayer partners Nancy McLoughlin, Esmirna "Mimi" Malave-Saavedra, Mireya Aguilar, and Carole Parrott Drew, I love you all. My very first Bible study group turned into a sisterhood. You allowed me to lead, and I have grown in my relationship with God. Marti Le Noir and Yolanda "Kitty" Mancuso, I am grateful for our countless conversations of God's goodness many hours after church service had ended. Tonia Lovelace & Rochelle Miles, God brought you two at the perfect time of my life. I respect and love you both. Jerry Medy, I love your desire for many, especially family, to know God. Thank you for your prayers for the book. I know God is pleased with your heart posture. To my inner circle who keeps me laughing and praying, whom I can count on for anything: Regine Cheeks, Macary Fils-Aime, Judith Celestin, Ruby Noble, Alexandra Shim-Chim, Rachelle Tomlinson and Beagy Fils-Aime. And, to my godmother, Jeannine Martelly, you have been a gift to me in my life. I love you all immensely.

Cheryl Fletcher and Kathy Christopher, your years of obedience impacted my relationship with God the Father, Son, and Holy Spirit; forever grateful. My Christian Assembly community informed my leadership and service to the glory of God! Tom Hughes, thank you for your obedience to grant me an opportunity to pastor. I learned so much! Mentors Sarah Dornbos "sè mwen," Paul Gibson, Doug and Sandy Lee Schaupp, you all talk the talk and walk the walk. You live out what it looks like to be a follower of Christ. You encourage and challenge others to do so from example. I am grateful for the opportunities given to be bold for the glory of God.

A special thank you to Cheryl Allen, Cheryl Fletcher, Julie Boit, Blythe Hill, Sandy Schaupp and Colie Kreuger, who immediately said yes to offering their gift of encouragement by their endorsements. I am continually encouraged by your boldness and courage to do what God has placed on your heart. May your cup overflow with God's goodness!

My husband, Dewain Robinson, our 31 years of partnership through life, has taught me priceless lessons that have shaped me as a wife, mother, God's daughter and servant.

Finally, a special thanks to Kayla Fils-Aime, Ruby Noble, and Judith Celestin, who gave the gift of their talents to the success of this book. Thank you to Marcia Jeffers, Lillian Castillo, Lisa Dizon, Debra K., Ruby N.,

Alexandra S., Diana N., Paola S., Tonia L., Rochelle M., and Marti L. for giving me valuable feedback on the book with very little notice. Love you all!

May God continue to be glorified through this book! May this book draw many to see themselves the way God sees them and be compelled to act.

PREFACE

And my message and my preaching were very plain. Rather than using clever and persuasive speeches, I relied only on the power of the Holy Spirit. I did this so you would trust not in human wisdom but in the power of God. Yet when I am among mature believers, I do speak with words of wisdom, but not the kind of wisdom that belongs to this world or to the rulers of this world, who are soon forgotten.

1 Corinthians 2: 4-6 (NLT)

One thing I'm sure of is that my words alone are shallow without the power of the Holy Spirit. I have peppered them with my own stories, along with real-world stories to encourage, inspire, and empower but all fall short to the power of God's word. No other words written under heaven and on earth can ever compare to the inerrant scripture written through man and breathed by God. My intent with this book is to encourage, inspire, and empower you to seek God's face in all things considering YOU. If you gain that longing and desire, then I've done my job. I celebrate with you! Press into the One who has created you with such purpose. He Himself has a purpose, which is revealed in this scripture,

> *Now when it was day, He departed and went into a deserted place. And the crowd sought Him and came to Him, and tried to keep Him from leaving them; but He said to them, "I must preach the kingdom of God to the other cities also, because for this purpose I have been sent."*
>
> Luke 4:42-43 NKJV

Jesus knows His purpose given to Him by the Father who sent Him. Everything He did from teaching, healing and so much more was always done with the intent to point His people to the Kingdom of God. The Kingdom of God is at hand. And from this place, we will seek to identify our unique purpose from the One who placed it there for His glory and His Kingdom.

> *"You are the salt of the earth. But what good is salt if it has lost its flavor? Can you make it salty again? It will be thrown out and trampled underfoot as worthless. You are the light of the world—like a city on a hilltop that cannot be hidden. No one lights a lamp and then puts it under a basket. Instead, a*

lamp is placed on a stand, where it gives light to everyone in the house."

Matthew 5:14-15 NLT

Let your light shine so His glory may be seen and felt by many. I will encourage you to self-reflection on the things that threatened to dampen your light, whether they were imposed on you when you were a child by the systems of this world, or by you willingly adopting the false narratives offered by this world that are contrary to who God says you are and the plans He has for your life.

I will lean on the term "purpose" because, for me, it suggests that you were born and created with intent. Most everything created by human hands has a purpose, from a toothbrush, spoon, and chair to the many types of screws that exist, depending on what you plan on building or creating. In the same way, everything God created has an intent and purpose. You, too, were created with a clear intent from the One who created you. My prayer and hope is that more of God's people will join the ranks of those who have gained clarity and understanding of that for which they've been created. I'm sure you can spot those few people who are operating in what they were clearly born to do. May there be more!

My purpose is to give you permission and encouragement to let your light shine before the world, so that

God gets the glory. Through guided self-reflections and prompts, you will discover with your Triune God more of what you were created for before the noise of this world brought confusion. Through moments of stillness, you'll be invited to develop an ear to discern the voice of your Triune God and accept the invitation to join in this most Holy union in relationship. What a humbling invitation to join! You may even think you're unworthy of the invitation. That invitation to partner with God may seem to be reserved for someone else more qualified by the partnership. I'm here to tell you that the invitation is for you. Yes, you! So hold out your hand and allow yourself to be led by the Holy Spirit, the one who is waiting to lead you.

I'm humbled that you would entrust me to guide you on your journey of exploration and discovery toward the things you've been uniquely created for. I celebrate with you and am excited to be a part. May our God show you wonderful things and may He heal you of burdens so you can be fully available to be used for His glory.

As you embark on this journey, I invite you not to censor yourself but, rather allow yourself to be vulnerable with a surrendered heart to the One who is trustworthy, for He already knows every hidden thing. Travel well!

Giving thanks,
Shirley Charles-Robinson

PART 1

AWAKE:

"The Lord came and stood there, calling as at the other times, "Samuel! Samuel!" Then Samuel said, "Speak, for your servant is listening."

1 Samuel 3:7-11 NIV

ARISE TO THE CALL

It Is No Accident

The fact that you're reading this book is no accident; no matter how this book has come into your hands, I pray that it will be the catalyst for God's plans uniquely purposed for your life. Countless prayers have gone out for the person who would one day hold this book, and that person is you! My prayer is that this book will motivate you to be courageous and, above all, obedient to what you were made for and created to do for the good of the Kingdom of God. Being obedient is easier said than done when you're being challenged with the daily responsibilities of life calling for your attention. So, I pray that despite the demands of life or the unexpected obstacles waiting for you, you'll persevere, even though they may seem like a mountain you cannot seem to overcome or climb. We'll dispel the thought that it's impossible to overcome any obstacle before us because we know we serve a God who will strengthen, sustain, and equip us for every situation. "I can do all things through Christ who strengthens me" (Philippians 4:13 NKJV). Do we believe this great truth, people of God?! This powerful verse in the Bible can be a lovely scripture to quote, but do we really believe that we serve a God who will equip us for every battle, whether in lack or in plenty, so that we can thrive and gain contentment despite any circumstance?

Let me be transparent with my own fears, doubts, and insecurities that have their roots from my ancestry, upbringing, culture, and environment. I understand and know these emotions well. These unhelpful emotions have delayed promises that God whispered to me many years ago, and that's why I'm well-suited to encourage you and challenge you to do it anyway. I hope that as you take this journey with me, you'll identify and operate more in the work you were called to and preserved for even before taking your first breath. The Bible is filled with numerous accounts of God depositing a calling in the hearts of people, and because of their obedience, He is able to do great things through them.

Moses comes immediately to mind. I feel a special kinship to Moses because I see myself in him. His humanness threatens to circumvent his very reason for being; the purpose he was reserved and preserved to accomplish. The work he was predestined to accomplish was staring him in the face as God called him forth from the burning bush. The call that was on Moses' life didn't begin at the burning bush; it started long before that pivotal moment. Unbeknownst to Moses, God had been preserving, providing, and equipping him long before he even took his first breath. It wasn't by accident that the Hebrews midwives, Shiphrah and Puah, made the conscious decision to preserve Moses' life and defy the king of Egypt's decree to kill all newborn Hebrew baby boys, which preserved Moses' life. It wasn't by accident that Moses' mom, Jochebed, saw that the son she bore was a "fine child," so she risked hiding him for three months and then made the most challenging decision that a mother can make, which is to release her child into the unknown world so that he can live. I wonder what Jochebed was thinking as she made the decision to let him go. As a mother, I know it required a lot of trust on her part. Did she possess an unwavering faith that her God would protect her baby? Or did she just hope for the best? According to scripture, she was a Levi. Levites were musicians, gate keepers, guardians, Temple officials, judges, and craftsmen, so I think we can deduce that her faith in the God of Abraham, Isaac, and Jacob enabled her to trust God. Imagine the trust it required for her to place Moses, her baby boy, in a basket made of papyrus reeds held together with bitumen and pitch, not sturdy materials, to be placed in the Nile River among crocodiles, snakes, and hippos. It wasn't by accident or luck that Moses, the baby, arrived at his intended destination unharmed; it was with great intentionality that he was able to find his final resting place near where Pharaoh's daughter would be bathing. It wasn't by accident that Pharaoh's daughter's decided to bathe in the Nile River banks and her heart was softened for this Hebrew baby boy who was condemned to die by her own father's decree. It wasn't by accident she decided to spare his life. It wasn't by accident that Miriam, Moses' sister, followed him and was prompted to ask Pharaoh's daughter if she could get a Hebrew woman (Jochebed) to be a nursemaid for Moses. I think we can safely say that it was no coincidence, luck, or happenstance; it was God from beginning to end using people's choices whether good or bad to fulfill His masterplan.

STEPS OF FAITH

- I want you to reflect on and write down a moment in your life that, in retrospect, you can attribute to God guiding your steps or preserving you from calamity.
- Are you able to see the impact that His Sovereign hand has on your life as well as the lives touched by yours, if so, how?
- Take a moment to thank God for His providence and for preserving you when you didn't know He was. Let this be a reminder that He is a God worthy of your trust.

PART 1

Obedience in Purpose

I was told that, as a baby, my mother traveled with me from the United States to Haiti to visit family, and, while we were there, I almost died. While I don't know the specifics of what caused this near-death experience, I like to think I was preserved to make an impact on society. I believe we're all preserved for a purpose. While we all may not have a grand calling like Moses, we all have a call, purpose, or mission, whether great or small. The midwives had a call to preserve as many Hebrew boys from annihilation as possible. Moses' mother had a call to preserve and raise Moses to be the man he would soon be called to be. Even Pharaoh's daughter had a call to preserve Moses' life. With each call, there's a moment of decision to answer it. These moments often are unique to our talent, abilities, or influence. They're opportunities, whether we realize it or not, to accomplish a purpose to give God glory. The Hebrew midwives could have obeyed Pharaoh's decree to kill all male newborns, but they feared God more. Moses' mother could have succumbed to the inevitable demise of her son, yet she decided to trust God for her son's preservation. Your purpose may require you to take the least likely position. Are you willing to take that step of faith? I believe you are!

We discover Moses being presented with a Kairos moment. A moment that unveils his purpose aside from him being husband and dad. An assignment uniquely designed to his unique background, talents, personality, and abilities. In the following passage of scripture, we gain insight into Moses' reluctance to answer God's call on his life. His reluctance was shrouded in insecurities, fears, contentment with his safe life, mixed with the need to gain the validation of humankind, resulting in downright disobedience.

In Exodus Chapter 3, God reveals Moses' assignment. God gives Moses unprecedented insight into the opposition he will encounter with Pharaoh as he leads the Israelites out of Egypt, as well as his inevitable victory in Egypt and over Pharoah. You would have thought the fact that God tells him he will be victorious would have been enough for him to say with confidence, "Well, let's go!" God essentially gives Moses the playbook; the cheat sheet. Yet, Moses proceeds to respond to God with a lot of what ifs and buts, which translates to self-centeredness, distrust and plain ignorance to the Sovereignty and Power of the I AM God he's communicating with.

Exodus Chapter 4 gives us deeper insight into Moses' heart, brand-new relationship with God, as well as God's patience and understanding for Moses' deficiencies and great potential.

> *Then Moses said to the Lord, "Please, Lord, I have never been eloquent, neither recently nor in time past, nor since*

PART 1

Thou hast spoken to Thy servant; for I am slow of speech and slow of tongue." And the Lord said to him, "Who has made man's mouth? Or who makes {him} dumb or deaf, or seeing or blind? Is it not I, the Lord? Now then go, and I, even I, will be your mouth, and teach you what you are to say."

(Exodus 4:10–12) —NASB

As I reflect on Moses' heart posture and response to God, his focus was on "me, me, me." Moses begins to list all the reasons why he's a horrible choice for this assignment, how God is making a mistake, and he needs to convince God of that, forgetting that God doesn't make mistakes. It may not always make sense to us, but all God is looking for is an obedient heart, and He will do the rest. As I mentioned before, this is why I feel such a kinship to Moses, because I had had similar conversations with God, even when I knew quite well that He was directing me to an assignment. Still, all my insecurities, masked by fear, were really about me not wanting to look foolish; I didn't want to allow my flaws to be exposed. I preferred to let my carefully crafted safe façade be left alone. Also, to be honest, it requires less work and less of me. This mindset robs us of the opportunity to see God's glory working in us and through us.

I'm reminded of another individual who disregarded the Sovereignty of the Almighty God. In the first chapter of Jonah, Jonah is called by God to arise and warn Nineveh about their evil deeds. Jonah arose, not to go to Nineveh, 725 miles away, but to flee to Tarshish, over 3,000 miles away. Jonah's disobedience was intentional. His heart posture was also self-centered. While Moses' disobedience was self-centeredness masked by fear, insecurities, and the approval of humankind, Jonah's disobedience was a self-centeredness rooted in his desire to withhold God's love and forgiveness from those who needed it the most. Jonah chose to dismiss God's assignment because He knew God would rescue the Ninevites whom he preferred to keep lost and suffer the judgment of God. Whether the disobedience is blatant like Jonah's or masked by our insecurities like Moses, it's all disobedience. Their self-centeredness could have sabotaged God's plan to rescue His creation, yet nothing and no one can thwart God's masterplan. Instead, God disrupts Jonah's trip and redirects him. God mercifully places Jonah in the belly of a whale for a while for incubation. During that incubation period, God developed within Jonah humility and a softened and obedient heart. I too have experienced incubation periods that were so hard that it caused me to cry out to the Lord. I've learned lessons in these times of incubation; you may call it a "valley" that God is using to develop us. God loves His children and servants too much to allow them to go astray. I've come to recognize these incubation periods and have learned to embrace them because I know there's a realignment that needs to happen within me that cannot occur otherwise, and in return, God sharpens me, humbles me, corrects me, and equips me in ways that I didn't know I needed. If you should find yourself in an incubation period, ask God what He desires from you. It won't be easy, but you'll be all the better for it; great things can be developed in you if you allow it.

Our disobedience may even surface as fear and doubt. Did I hear what I thought I heard? In Judges 6: 36-40 (NKJV),

> Gideon said to God, "If You will save Israel by my hand as You have said— look, I shall put a fleece of wool on the threshing floor; if there's dew on the fleece only, and it is dry on all the ground, then I shall know that You will save Israel by my hand, as You have said." And it was so. When he rose early the next morning and squeezed the fleece together, he wrung the dew out of the fleece, a bowlful of water. Then Gideon said to God, "Do not be angry with me, but let me speak just once more: Let me test, I pray, just once more with the fleece; let it now be dry only on the fleece, but on all the ground let there be dew." And God did so that night. It was dry on the fleece only, but there was dew on all the ground.

Gideon starts by saying, "If." He reveals his potential disobedience is surfacing as doubt. He's not sure he heard God correctly. Again, the shift is away from God's Sovereignty and inward. Gideon wants proof that God is going to do what He said He will do. At first glance, you might wonder what's wrong with Gideon making sure he's hearing God right. Maybe Gideon's ear isn't developed enough to discern God's voice like young Samuel. In 1 Samuel Chapter 3, Samuel, a young boy assisting Eli in the temple, heard God's voice and thought it was Eli calling for him. He didn't know it was God calling him until Eli told him the voice he heard was God's. However, with further investigation that's not what was happening with Gideon. We see that earlier in Chapter 6 of Judges, God directs Gideon to pull down the altar of Baal. Gideon hears God clearly and executes God's instruction with no hesitation or doubt, but proceeds to do it in fear of men in verse 27,

> So Gideon took ten men from among his servants and did as the Lord had said to him. But because he feared his father's household and the men of the city too much to do it by day, he did it by night." And when the men of the city arose early in the morning, there was the altar of Baal, torn down; and the wooden image that was beside it was cut down, and the second bull was being offered on the altar which had been built. So they said to one another, "Who

PART 1

has done this thing?" And when they had inquired and asked, they said, "Gideon the son of Joash has done this thing." Then the men of the city said to Joash, "Bring out your son, that he may die, because he has torn down the altar of Baal, and because he has cut down the wooden image that was beside it."

This experience prompted Gideon's doubt because he had interaction with God prior to testing God with the fleece. This experience scared him. He wanted assuredness before he obeyed.

Allow me to be transparent and reveal my deficiencies without judgment. I've been like Moses, Jonah, and Gideon at one point or another. I have had moments when my fears and insecurities surfaced like Moses. I doubted I heard God correctly and tested God like Gideon. I also stood on the sidelines like Jonah, waiting for those to suffer the consequences and judgment of their actions. How does your disobedience tend to reveal itself when you're called? Are you most like Moses, Jonah, or Gideon?

This book is birthed out of my journey as a wife of twenty-three years and mother of four beautiful children in the midst of all of life's responsibilities, trials, setbacks of all kinds, and, of course, joys. I found myself in an incubation period. My marriage, personal relationships with family, finances, and home life were in total disarray. Amid the chaos in my life, God was depositing this book on my heart and a pastoral apprenticeship, which I knew was God-ordained. I prayed, "God, come back when my life is calmer; come when there's more order. God, my life is a mess now!" We won't be able to control when God calls, and His timing could be less than desirable to us, but perfect because it challenges us to hold unto Him and rely on Him. I want you to remember that God doesn't make mistakes, and His timing is perfect. It hasn't been easy. At times, I had so much opposition in the natural and spiritual realm. It seemed like this book would remain an idea prompted to me by the Holy Spirit but never to be fully realized.

I share this all to say that what God is calling you to will be filled with much opposition from outside elements as well as internal turmoil. This book was birthed out of insecurities, doubt, fear, unbelief, belief, faith, power, and obedience. I'm thankful that belief, faith, and obedience won over the insecurities, doubt, and fear. I hope that encourages you. Oftentimes, we see the success and victories of others, a finished product that's all nice and polished, but we don't get to see the pain, tears, and uncertainty that preceded the victory. My hope is that you'll find comfort and realize that, in spite of your fears, doubts, and whatever you carry, God wants to work something more profound in you than the calling He has put on your life. He wants to prune you, sharpen you, and invite you to a relation-

PART 1

ship dependent on Him and Him alone.

I want you to know you're not alone in running this race that has been set before you (Hebrews 12:1-3). God will equip you with the courage, tools, resources, finances, and divine appointments necessary to accomplish His perfect plan in you and through you. All you have to do is trust Him, believe that He placed the passion and desire in you, and He will equip you with all that's necessary. Do you believe it? I pray that you do. Even if you don't fully believe it, take a step forward anyway toward obedience; after all, that's what faith is all about. It's belief, trust, and hope in the One who can do miraculous things that we can't comprehend. *"But hope that is seen is not hope; for who hopes for what he already sees? But if we hope for what we don't see, with perseverance we wait eagerly for it"* (Romans 8:24-25 NASB). The hope referred to in this passage is the hope we Christians hope for in our bodies' redemption. I believe we can apply this kind of hope in the calling that God has whispered to us individually what we haven't yet seen come into fruition. Faith isn't in our own abilities but in what God, the Creator of Heaven and Earth, can do through us and for us. For that, I'm thankful! I keep reminding myself it's not up to me and not about me. He will remove the obstacles needed to be removed, but for the purposes of sharpening me in the fire, some of these obstacles will remain. This reminded me of Paul's petition to God to remove this unknown obstacle and

God kept responding to him, *"My grace is all you need. My power works best in weakness."* So now I am glad to boast about my weaknesses, so that the power of Christ can work through me (2 Corinthians 12: 9 NLT)

I love Paul's response. I'll boast about my weakness all the more. We live in a society where you're convinced to hide your weaknesses and don't admit to your weaknesses. Instead, you portray this false façade and air that you're free of any weaknesses and have it all together, when you know deep inside that you're trying, in your humanness, to hold everything together, and, at any moment, it will all fall apart. God's power magnified in our weakness is a humbling concept to embody; our surrendered weakness is the very thing that allows God to shine; not that He needs us to shine, but so we can stand in utter awe at what He is able to do in us and through us. It reminds us that whatever we're pursuing is ultimately for our good, but more importantly, for the good of all humankind and the Glory of God. I don't know about you, but a weight is lifted off me as I acknowledge this truth. I don't need to feel like I have it all figured out or have all the skills and resources needed because our God will provide and equip us with what's needed when we need it. I love that the staff that Moses already had in his possession was used on his journey in Egypt. God allowed that staff to be transformed to what Moses needed when he needed it. He equipped him for the journey, and He will do the same for you. He gives us what we need before we even know we need it. *"I'll answer them before they even call to me. While they're still talking about their needs, I'll go ahead and answer their prayers!" (Isaiah 65:24 NLT).* That's our God! You should feel great comfort and hope that God steps in before we even call to Him. It does for me! Before I ask or complete my sentence, He has set a plan in motion for my good and the good of His creation. That's what happened at the Garden of Eden when Adam and Eve disobeyed God and were cast out. God sets a plan in motion before we even know a plan is needed. That's our God! He is a rescuer! He sounds the trumpet and immobilizes the cavalry of heaven's angels to bring about victory.

As someone who struggles with control in various areas of my life, God is constantly challenging me to release the reins to Him. This was truly a challenge for me. At an early age, I learned to rely on no one else but myself to get things done. In fact, my mom taught me to be self-sufficient. I internalized this to mean, don't ask for help; don't bother people; figure it out on your own! This thinking is partly cultural. However, I also suspect she experienced disappointments from loved ones who simply came up short. I learned quickly in my adult life that no one makes it on their own. You need to trust and rely on other people, of course, with wisdom, but the alternative leaves you all alone trying to push a boulder up the mountain. Having some trusted people in your life to help you move the boulder up the mountain is so much more doable and can even be fun when you're doing it in community. In the same way, God wants us to partner with Him; lean on Him; trust Him, and, most importantly, surrender EVERYTHING to Him. Please, by "surrender," I don't mean you should throw your hands up in the air, doing nothing; I'm referring to the surrendering of your doubts, insecurities, and your own abilities, knowing that God will equip and provide the increase. As I learned what the relationship with the I AM God requires, which isn't an overnight journey, my ability to surrender in trust has strengthened. My ability to believe and remain faithful in obedience has become more of a norm than not. More and more, I'm coming to a place of surrender of will and self-sufficiency to trust the One who is All Sufficient. I don't want to give this false impression that it's an easy journey; in fact, I came to this place, not always willingly. I guess I hit enough walls trying to do it my way that I realized His ways are simply better than my ways.

When Moses finally succumbed to God's call to lead the Israelites out of Egypt, his success was dependent on his complete submission to God. Even though I know this is necessary in my own life, it doesn't mean I won't try to take up the reins of control, and my own wisdom kicks back in, and I pick up the weight of perfection, the pursuit of success at all cost and approval of man: a weight I wasn't designed to carry. I attribute it in part to my Haitian culture and upbringing, being raised by a strong mother, who had to be strong due to society and environmental realities. I can only imagine what she endured as a young woman who immigrated from Haiti to a country that was foreign to her. My mom had to learn very quickly how to adapt and assimilate in order to experience the financial freedom that she heard the United States offered. Our Western culture and philosophy of picking "ourselves up by our bootstraps," or putting "our big girl panties on," "self-made," "self-taught," etc. permeates our way of thinking. In fact, it's applauded. I'm sure you heard all those catchphrases at least once in your life. I embodied this kind of thinking. The thinking that it all depends on me to make it happen. All I managed to do was spin my wheels, doing everything with my own strength, wondering why I kept hitting a wall in exhaustion.

I most likely will have to remind myself to give it back to God, because I'm constantly reminding myself to let go of the reins and stop carrying the weight I wasn't designed or created to carry. I hope you didn't miss a keyword in that last sentence, "reminding." It's interesting to me, but intentional, God repeatedly tells the Israelites in the desert, in the book of Exodus, to either do something in remembrance of an event that occurred or to remember what He has already done. He knows His people. We, unfortunately, have short-term memory. We forget His promises, His character, and His love for us. I don't think we'll fully comprehend this love until we find ourselves basking in His presence.

Take note; you'll need to remind yourself of what's true and what's possible with God many times. For a time, I found it necessary to be part of a recovery group, and in that recovery that was non-faith based, they knew that it was necessary to have a divine power greater than themselves to overcome their particular struggle. I encourage you to form a group of trusted individuals that you'll need to help you remind yourself of what, I hope, you already know about our God. Why? Because we often rely on what we see, and what we see can seem discouraging and impossible. In those moments, you'll need to remind yourself of what you know to be true and even go to those trusted advocates to remind you of such truth, so you won't be tempted to throw in the towel. It will have to be a faith muscle that you exercise until it becomes stronger. Otherwise, you get frustrated when you believe the very thing that's possible is impossible.

My journey toward weight loss often led me to believe that I had too many things working against me: metabolism, age, time, finances, etc. I longed for the days when I didn't have to worry about what I put in my mouth and how much of it I put in my mouth; I could simply consume and enjoy it. Those days are no more.

I would gain strides and lose them just as quickly, which left me frustrated. I had to remind myself of what was possible when my inclination was to revert to old habits that didn't serve me well. It wasn't long before I realized that it would be a battle that I'll have to engage daily to maintain the healthy weight that would serve my height and age well. I had to be intentional and mindful that this was the way I would need to conduct myself in order to gain the desired goal and retain it! I must be honest that I have experienced seasons when the pull of a dessert—who am I kidding—the pull of multiple visits to tempting desserts won over and derailed my progress. I had to decide to get back up again and stay the course. Even though I had a setback, I had to make the decision not to throw in the towel but reengage and do the things that I knew that would maintain my commitment.

I want you to be sober minded about the journey you'll embark on. Those habits and thought processes that haven't served you well or you thought were conquered will try to rear their ugly heads. You'll have to be intentional and create a process that carries you through those moments of fear and insecurities that will seek to derail you. Together, in the coming chapters, we'll set on a journey to create a system that, hopefully, won't allow you to be your worst enemy. One of the most important systems we're going to develop is the ability to recognize God's voice in obedience. My hope is that you'll save precious time spinning your wheels, doing everything but what God has uniquely created you to do and self-sabotaging yourself in the process.

The goal of this book is to awaken those God whispers that lie dormant in the recesses of your mind and heart; identify why they were left dormant; gain clarity, encouragement, and power from the One who empowers; and apply actionable steps to bring this purpose forth so that All may benefit. Your gifts and purpose aren't for you alone, but to edify those in your sphere of influence and ultimately give God glory.

To God be the glory!

You're made with purpose for a purpose!

PART II

RECONSTRUCTION:

Then they will rebuild the ancient ruins,
They will raise up the former devastations;
And they will repair the ruined cities,
The desolations of many generations.

Isaiah 61:4

PREPARING FOR THE JOURNEY

Let's take this journey of discovering what God planned for your life when He was knitting you in your mother's womb. *"You made all the delicate, inner parts of my body and knit me together in my mother's womb" (Psalm 139:13 NLT).* I don't know much about knitting other than the knitter is intentional; they have a plan already in mind as to what they'll make and how they'll make it. They've identified what they'll make, the color, the texture of the yarn, the type of stitch, and the tools that will be needed. God did something similar in the way He created you. Nothing about how He has made you is a mistake. He was intentional about the way he made your nose, the shape of your eyes, your height, stature, the texture and color of your hair, etc. He created not only the outer parts but also the inner parts of your body. And beyond your physical attributes, God has made YOU with great Purpose according to His likeness.

Then God said, "Let Us make man in Our image, according to Our likeness:" [We're made in His likeness. I don't think we'll fully understand the breadth of that statement until we see Him face to face. Nonetheless, we're His image bearers very much like we bear the likeness of our parents in physical attributes, and mannerisms. God didn't stop there. He made us and then He gave us a purpose, an assignment to complete.] "and let them have dominion over the fish of the sea, over the birds of the air, and over the cattle, over all the earth and over every creeping thing that creeps on the earth." So, God created man in His own image; in the image of God, He created him; male and female He created them. Genesis 1:26-27 NKJV)

Our God created you with all your talents, abilities, strengths, characteristics, and personal stories with great purpose and intentionality to be used not only to benefit yourself but to benefit others. God knows what the world He has created needs, which is you in the way God has fashioned you. Our societies tend to want to set standards of what's beautiful, acceptable, and worthy. And we sadly fall for these false narratives. Why do we do that? I've done it for a great deal of my life until I learned about my true identity from the One who created me. Once I began to learn and embrace the truth from the One who made me, the shackles of this world started to fall away one by one. The shackles of approval, beauty, acceptance, and validation no longer had a hold over me like it once did. Read this love message to you from your Creator from Psalm 139: 15- 18 BSB:

> I praise You, for I am fearfully and wonderfully made. Marvelous are Your works, and I know this very well. My frame was not hidden from You when I was made in secret, when I was woven together in the depths of the earth. Your eyes saw my unformed body; all my days were written in Your book and ordained for me before one of them came to be. How precious to me are Your thoughts, O God, how vast is their sum! If I were to count them, they would outnumber the grains of sand; and when I awake, I am still with You.

Our God delights in you. No matter what your story may hold. He loves you! You may say, "If you only knew.... No one can love someone like me." You may have a hard time loving yourself for whatever reason. Or someone may have led you to believe you're not worth loving. I'm here to tell you that those reasons can never supersede God's love for you and what He says about you. He says nothing can separate you from Him. Whatever circumstance you may experience at any given time that may make you think He has abandoned you, embrace this scripture and repeat it until you believe that despite your circumstance when His presence seems so far, He is a God who will never leave you or forsake you,

> *Can anything ever separate us from Christ's love? Does it mean he no longer loves us if we have trouble or calamity, or are persecuted, or hungry, or destitute, or in danger, or threatened with death? (As the Scriptures say, "For your sake we are killed every day; we are being slaughtered like sheep.") No, despite all these things, overwhelming victory is ours through Christ, who loved us. And I am convinced that nothing can ever separate us from God's love. Neither death nor life, neither angels nor demons, neither our fears for today nor our worries about tomorrow—not even the powers of hell can separate us from God's love. No power in the sky above or in the earth below—indeed, nothing in all creation will ever be able to separate us from the love of God that is revealed in Christ Jesus our Lord.*
>
> (Romans 8: 35-39 NLT)

Adam and Eve were formed with great purpose and intentionality. He didn't haphazardly make them just for His whim. He invited Adam and Eve with a purpose and a partnership to what He created.

> *Then God blessed them, and God said to them, "Be fruitful and multiply; fill the earth and subdue it; have dominion*

PART II

> *over the fish of the sea, over the birds of the air, and over every living thing that moves on the earth."*
>
> Genesis 1:28 NKJV)

Their partnership with God allowed them to have access and ownership to the things He created and the assignment to fill it, subdue it, and have dominion over it. Imagine the person you most respect and admire comes to you directly and invites you to partner with them. How would that make you feel? For me, it would be Nelson Mandela if he were still alive. I respect and admire his resilience, sacrifice, wisdom, boldness, and impact on our world. If he were to call me and say, "Shirley, I would like you to partner with me." I would feel a great sense of honor, humility, and pride that someone of his stature would trust me with his important work. A more tangible figure for me today would be Stacey Abrams. She is like a female version of Martin Luther King in her determination despite the odds. Despite her gubernatorial loss in Georgia, she was intent on making sure every American's vote would be unhindered. The stakes are high, but she doesn't allow herself to be dismayed or deterred; in fact, she allows the stakes to fuel her perseverance. And she perseveres towards victory. I see this less a political win but more of a humanitarian win. A call from her I would receive with honor. Well, God is that very important person. The Creator of the universe is saying He entrusts you with His creation. So, what did He entrust you with? Think of the things and people that God has allowed you to have access, influence, and leadership over. It could be your marriage, children, friendships, business, relationships, employees, community, property, or a cause. How does that make you feel? Do you feel drunk with power? Or do you feel an immense sense of responsibility drenched with humility and honor? I hope you feel humbled and honored by the trust that God has given you. I remember when leaving the maternity ward for the first time. I was overwhelmed with excitement and responsibility. My husband and I were being allowed to take our perfect baby girl devoid of any blemish or trauma to nurture and develop. It was a humbling experience to know that we were responsible for this life. We did our best to give her the best possible chance for a full and thriving life by eating the right things during pregnancy and creating the best environment for her development. In the first years of her life, I felt an incredible responsibility that she meet all her milestones of development. She was my assignment, my purpose. Since then, I've come to understand my purpose beyond being a mother and wife and all that God has entrusted me with to include the passions He has placed inside me to edify others and reflect His glory.

If you're clear on your purpose, your assignment from God, then I celebrate with you. You're well on your journey toward obedience. However, knowing your assignment isn't the same as doing the assignment. We see this with Jonah in Jonah 1:2. He was given a clear assignment by God but chose not to complete his assignment. Hopefully, this journey will confirm and reaffirm what God has whispered to you and spur you toward action.

If you're unclear and have no clue about what your purpose, your assignment, could be, don't fret! Instead, I encourage you to take this journey with excitement to discover what your Creator's unique plan is for you. I'll provide opportunities along the way to develop the ability to hear from God and moments to self-reflect on your past story to discover what it can teach you so you gain clarity, but the most crucial piece of the puzzle is action. It's not enough to know. You must take what you know and do something with it. A diploma of any kind is just a piece of paper until you make that paper work for you in a tangible way. A dream, an idea, or a mandate from God will remain just that until it becomes a tangible experience through action.

So, let's begin to build a firm foundation that will withstand life's challenges. God's Word says, "*I have told you these things, so that in me you may have peace. In this world you will have trouble. But take heart! I have overcome the world*" *(John 16:33 NLT)* The trials and tribulations that Jesus refers to in this passage of scripture are speaking to the persecution that His people will one day endure through bodily harm or death. However, we can gain some encouragement today from this scripture. While currently, we, in the United States, don't experience persecution, you can still gain the peace offered. You'll experience trouble and opposition of all forms that will try to prevent you from moving forward with the things that God has laid on your heart, but don't despair, for God is with you. Don't think that there isn't an enemy of God intent on derailing the plans that God is calling you to.

In the book of Exodus, Moses experienced enormous opposition from Pharaoh's unwillingness to let Israel worship God and the Israelites unwillingness to trust God's plan. The opposition he encountered would have discouraged most and caused many to throw in the towel. If I were in his shoes, I would have said, "This is too much! I'm outta here!" Thankfully for us, he persevered amid opposition from Pharoah from the very people he was called to lead out of slavery, he remained obedient to his assignment, his purpose.

You'll set out to build a momentum that will carry you through when "life happens" and the opposition is insurmountable, so you won't be tempted to throw in the towel and retreat. I experienced a form of opposition that was of my own making, in some cases. It surfaced as distraction, poor time-management, doubt, strained finances, fear, exhaustion, etc. Does any of this resonate with you? All these things can tempt you to doubt God's whispering in your heart and offer you reasonable excuses that will lead you to say, "This isn't the right time." And it may very well not be the right time. Have you said yes to things that prevent you from doing the very purpose that you say you want to do? That was my favorite! That reasonable excuse made it easy for me not to fail. How can you fail at something you never start? How can you commit to the very thing God is whispering to you if you keep yourself busy doing other useful things? Or maybe you said, "I don't have time," but you've managed to meet everyone else's needs or expectations.

Let me share how a series of unexpected events of my life almost caused me to be disobedient to my assignment from God. As I began taking actionable steps toward obedience, I sensed God was calling me to "life happened."

"Life happened," when I unexpectedly had five adult family members in the course of a year in need of help and lodging. So, I felt an obligation as well as a personal desire to extend support. After all, as Christ-followers, we're called to help those in need, right? However, I've now come to understand and learn how to approach this call to help in a healthier way that doesn't exclude God from doing the work He desires to do in the lives of our loved ones who need our help. I learned the tough but necessary lesson that the Holy Spirit is the only one who can do the restorative and redemptive work needed. I knew this in theory, but I didn't know how to live that out in my life. So, I did what was expected of me culturally and what I wanted to do because of my innate desire to help. After all, over my lifetime, I've been the recipient of the kindness and generosity of many who've helped me on my journey. How could I not extend the same kindness and generosity!? They're my family, after all! Family helps one another, right!? However, I allowed their situation to monopolize my life, which then became a distraction. I let their predicament cause me to put things to the side. I took on the role of rescuer. I got to fix this, so I believed! There's no way I could operate fully amid the disorder I created for myself. I graciously welcomed my family, whom I love, into my home ill-prepared for what happens when you haven't set forth strong, loving boundaries and expectations. As a result, this book took a back seat to the unexpected and expected "happenings of life."

"Life happened," when I found myself working two jobs. I was beyond exhausted and couldn't even fathom carving out time to do what I believed was a God-centered calling on my life.

"Life happened," when my finances hit an all-time low, and the stress of that alone led me to think that things were hopeless and impossible. That defeated thinking began to spill into the very thing God wanted to do through me.

During these "life happenings," God placed me in position to be invited to a Pastoral Apprenticeship that

PART II

I didn't set out to pursue, but God had other plans for me, so in obedience, I started marching toward the unknown. While it was full of challenges amid personal challenges God was sharpening me and refining me for the work He set before me.

"Life happened," when my family relationships were in chaos. Hence, the Holy Spirit prompted me to join a recovery group to get new tools and retire the old tools that may have served me well at one point in my life to cope with challenging situations. However, my coping mechanisms were no longer serving me well for the things that God was calling me to today.

"Life happened," when managing the day-to-day of raising four kids with one headed to college and one who's disinterested in school seemed more than I could bear.

And "life happened," when I realized my marriage required resuscitation or there wouldn't be one if careful attention weren't given to it. Yep, that was my life. Amid the roller coaster ride that was my life that felt chaotic and disorderly, I didn't see how writing a book was even possible. The timing of the call was less than ideal. All of this was happening simultaneously. Unbeknownst to me, there would be many more storms brewing and on the horizon as life can bring.

So how does one persevere beyond the storms, "life happenings" responsibilities, and curveballs while sensing a call? Guess what? If you're waiting for your calendar to be clear and your life to be free of curveballs!

Good luck! I'm writing this book as the world is contending with a pandemic. If that isn't a "life happening" or curve ball, I don't know what is. The pandemic can do one of two things: 1) cause you to put everything on pause and wait for things to return to normal (whatever that means), or 2) find a way to persevere amid this genuine challenge with the help of God.

I suggest a few ways to persevere beyond "life happenings":

1. INVITE

Invite God into your present situation, withhold nothing.

> Do not be anxious about anything, but in everything by prayer and supplication with thanksgiving let your requests be made known to God. And the peace of God, which surpasses all understanding, will guard your hearts and your minds in Christ Jesus. (Philippians 4:6–7)

Bring every burden, concern, confusion, and doubt to the foot of the throne of God. Our God delights when we invite Him into our lives. He is always available and patiently waiting for us to allow Him to be our "pillar by night" and "cloud by day." He was that for the Israelites when they were freed from captivity in Egypt, journeying in the wilderness to the promised destination. God was a pillar to the Israelites to light the way at night and a cloud to protect them from the scorching sun by day. That's the God who desires to lead the way for you and cover you while you do it. All you need to do is invite Him to be your guide. Your invitation to Him demonstrates that you acknowledge His sovereignty. It proves that you trust that He won't lead you astray, and He will provide all you need when you need it.

STEPS OF FAITH

- What are you wrestling with by yourself? What are you carrying that you need the intervention of a big and mighty God to intervene; to be your pillar of fire by night and a cloud by day?

2. SELF-EVALUATE

You're evaluated by others, such as an instructor or an employer, to assess your progress and abilities. I encourage you to do this for yourself. If it's foreign to you to self-evaluate yourself, I recommend making it part of your daily practice from now on. Ask God to give you understanding as you evaluate yourself. Look at behavioral patterns that may not be serving you well and are hindering you from wholeness. *"Trust in the*

LORD with all your heart, And lean not on your own understanding; In all your ways acknowledge Him, And He shall direct your paths" (Proverbs 3:5-6 NKJV).

Self-evaluating helps you to reflect on where you are and where you intend to go. It can illuminate how you operate in your work life and professional and personal relationships, how you respond to challenges, and a host of other things. When you find yourself at crossroads, I always recommend self-evaluating your past and current situation. This practice will offer you clarity. Clarity is key to everything. The more you're clear, the more effective you become. Again, invite God in this self-evaluation process, especially if you find yourself knocking your head against the same wall. I remember times I allowed my family to stay in my home, and it rarely ended the way I hoped. I envisioned hugs, gratitude, and celebration. Rather, it seemed to end with disappointments on both sides. As I tried to understand why I was always getting the same results, I soon realized that I didn't always establish clear expectations and consequences. Inviting God to help me self-evaluate the situation helped me get better in communicating clearer guidelines and boundaries.

STEPS OF FAITH

- Now that you've invited God to your situation, close your eyes and ask Him to help you take

honest self-evaluation and introspection in the areas of your life that are troublesome. Write it down.
- Ask God how you should proceed and handle this new information?
- Now act on the things He has spoken to you. Remember what He speaks to you will never be in contradiction to who He is. If your relationship is new, I implore you to go to someone who has a seasoned relationship with God for guidance.

3. LISTEN

We live in a society with nonstop noise and outside stimuli that overstimulate our eyes and ears. Our phones, TV, computers, texting, and social media are all good things; however, if you don't make a conscious choice to turn these things off, it will be hard to listen. What are we listening for? Well, we're listening for the voice of God. Throughout scripture, we see God is speaking to His creation. He sends angels. He speaks through visions and dreams. It seems that we tend to believe that the way God communicated is reserved only for those in the pages of the Bible, and it's not a possibility for us today. If you hold this thinking, I want to tell you the same God that told Abraham to leave his extended family and home to an unknown place is the same God who wants to speak to you today. *"My sheep* hear my voice, and I know them, and they follow me. I give them eternal life, and they will never perish, and no one will snatch them out of my hand" (John 10:27-28 ESV). He desires us to recognize His voice and a promise is attached when we recognize His voice. When He speaks to us, it's to bring us wholeness, protection, and eternal life. Why wouldn't we want to hear from a God who offers this as a promise? We seek after mentors, which is a good thing; however, we want the greatest mentor of them all as our guide, God. *"Call to me and I will answer you and tell you great and unsearchable things you do not know" (Jeremiah 33:3 NIV)*

The wonderful thing about our God is that He doesn't just want us to listen for His voice. He wants us to call on Him. This relationship is reciprocal. He wants to hear our voice too. Our voice is music to His ear. *"Then you will call on me and come and pray to me, and I will listen to you" (Jeremiah 29:12 NIV)*.

We need to know our Shepherd's voice. He wants us to know when He is speaking with us. I remember an incident at the beach when I was separated from my two younger sons. I frantically called for them, hoping they could hear and recognize my voice as I was listening for theirs. The only way we could recognize one another's voice is from time spent in each other's presence. I couldn't wait to be united with them and hear their voices. The only way we'll come to recognize our Shepherd's voice is spending time in His presence. However, we have to give Him space to do it. If all our senses, which should allow us to listen and hear His voice, are always overstimulated, then, yeah, it will be difficult to hear Him. When I was doing my graduate work and lived far away from all my family and friends, it was the most challenging time of my life. At that time, I lived alone and tended to fill my space with noise either from the TV or music. I didn't enjoy the silence because I didn't want to feel alone. We tend to fill our space with something to do, hear, and see. I imagine one of the reasons why Abraham and many in the Bible could hear God is because they didn't have all the distractions that we have to contend with today. The times that they lived in provided space to hear God. It allowed Joseph and Mary, and countless others to listen to what their Creator wanted them to know. I've led countless small groups over the years to the practice of silence; five minutes of silence seemed like an eternity. So, let's put this into practice. I want you to get a new journal or use the companion guide designed for this book and find a quiet place. This book is designed to be interactive. You want to not only read about the benefits of listening in silence but also incorporate it as part of your practice.

STEPS OF FAITH

- I recommend starting with a few minutes and gradually, over time, increase the time you set aside for silence until you can do it comfortably. This means no music, reading, or looking at anything, just complete silence. You determine your level of comfort. Schedule time for this and place it in your calendar. Before you know it, it will become part of your daily practice, especially when you need to hear from Him.

The ability to hear from God and the ability to know yourself is imperative. I implore you to INVITE God to give you discernment as to how to proceed. Sometimes, it will require you to persevere amid the "life happenings," and, sometimes, it may require you to pause everything and give your complete focus to the "life happenings." This is when you need the wisdom to Invite God into the situation, Self-Evaluate the situation, and assess your bandwidth to persevere. Not everyone is built the same. What one can overcome can break another. This is when knowing yourself will become so important, so you know how to handle these "life happenings" without disappointment, regret, guilt, or burnout. And then, give space for the Holy Spirit to guide you.

I remember a time in my life when God prompted me to pause and clear my calendar of specific activities. I didn't know why and, to be honest, I didn't want to. These good activities gave me purpose, so I thought. I felt accomplished. They provided me with healthy distractions, or were they!? I liked being busy with the kids. However, I knew this prompting was from God. For me, His voice wasn't audible, but for me, at that moment, it was the inner voice that I've come to recognize as the Holy Spirit leading me. So, I began to put certain activities on pause, such as my kids' vigorous basketball schedule and auditions. He wanted me to work on some enabling and codependency behaviors that weren't yielding fruit, so I shifted my focus to the inner work that I sensed was needed for my family and me. The foundation I created required some attention. It was necessary to put all these good things and even essential things on pause to chase after the restoration for me and my family that required healing to occur so we could be whole and thrive. I realized I kept my calendar busy with many worthwhile things that made it easy not to have time to do the inner work that would allow me to be more effective and identify the purpose for which I was created.

During my pastoral apprenticeship, I wanted to quit hundreds of times because my personal life was under reconstruction. God was moving me out of my comfort zone and removing people from my life. All of this was necessary, but change is uncomfortable even when it's not serving you well. Insecurities I thought were conquered seemed to be rearing their ugly heads. I called this period in my life "RECONSTRUCTION" because it felt, for me, like when your home is under renovation, and you're unable to move about your house like you're accustomed to. You can't access things easily. You have to make adjustments to your daily life that can be frustrating and annoying. You can't wait to feel unhindered once again, but you suffer through the renovation process because you know, in the end, it will all be worth it. The results will be worth all of the inconvenience you endured while the renovation was being done.

As I reflect and, in some cases, am still in the throes of these challenging situations, I realized that I might have gotten my book written and course launched, but I would have done it on a shaky foundation. That moment of pause God called me to that I didn't quite understand was designed to better prepare me to withstand all the obstacles and opposition. For me, it was a moment of refining that I didn't know I needed. I've come to be grateful for each of the "life happenings," these seemingly unexpected events, challenging situations, and delays. Did I want to go through these "life happenings?" Of course not, but these "life happenings" caused me to lean on God more. I reaped the wisdom that could only come from the various experiences, which have given me the perseverance to forge ahead when I felt like I was in a storm and didn't feel like the sun would come out. I've gained wisdom and maturity in ways that could only have come from going through the situations and leaning on God as I put one foot in front of the other. I believe what I endured has the potential to enrich everyone who holds this book in their hands. It was all part of God's refining process. I plan to be transparent with my shortcomings and trials because in these weaknesses, God's power can be magnified in and through me. At the time, I couldn't have imagined what felt like an unwelcome distraction filled with insurmountable pain and hardship could be used by God to sharpen me in the way He needed to prepare me for where He wanted to take me. So, if you find yourself in situations that may be wrought with pain, ask God, "What do You want me to learn or come away with for the better?"

STEPS OF FAITH

- I want you to take a moment to see where God may want to Reconstruct something different in you that you wouldn't choose for yourself? Where can this process help you fully be available for the purpose-designed for you? Write it down.
- Write down all the distractions, trials, lessons, and life responsibilities you currently face. How can you reframe these experiences to reap the growth that's possible?
- Pause to allow God to speak to you about the purpose of these seemingly unexpected distrac-

tions and trials. A lesson can be learned in them and be an unsuspecting gift.
- Now I want you to say, "Thank you!" Thank God for what your current situation taught you to sharpen in you more of His character that's useful for His purposes. God doesn't allow you to go through trials without intending to ultimately work them out for your good if you're courageous enough to let Him.

The developing phase of our character often can only be seen in retrospect. In Chapter 1 of James, James encourages the persecuted Christians by saying,

Consider it pure joy, my brothers and sisters, whenever you face trials of many kinds, because you know that the testing of your faith produces perseverance. Let perseverance finish its work so that you may be mature and complete, not lacking anything.

(James 1:2-4 NIV)

I don't believe I would have liked hearing this while being persecuted. Are you telling me I should find joy in the persecution? It doesn't make sense. Oh, but it does. In these challenging places, you emerge, bearing better, sweeter fruit. Often, we want strength; we ask God to strengthen us, but we don't like the lessons needed to build strength. We want wisdom, but we don't want to submit to the experiences that will produce wisdom. We want immovable faith, but we don't want to encounter situations that will test and build our faith. You could see where I'm going with this, right!? We want the harvest without the toil. So, I want you to shift your perspective to know what you can gain from what seems to be distractions, annoyances, delays, and obstacles. At the same time, some lessons are brought about from our own poor choices. Hopefully, as we get older through experience, we make fewer poor decisions and more of those that will serve us and humanity well.

We must not forget that some trials are outright tools of the enemy. However, we want to discern when it's not the work of the enemy and a direct result of poor planning or poor choices. It would be too easy to place the blame on our adversary, Satan, for every hardship, thereby absolving ourselves of responsibility for our present situation. Some hardships can be directly from our own decisions rooted in mismanagement and poor choices. So, what does it mean to discern? It means to have proper judgment about a situation; a person, or anything that requires you to make good choices. Let's be sober minded here. Again, as I mentioned, if this is, in fact, an assignment that God has prepared for you in advance, expect that you'll be met with opposition. The enemy doesn't want you to be successful. He doesn't want lives to be impacted and transformed for the Kingdom. Start by asking the Holy Spirit to help you discern which situation or history was due to poor choices and which ones were clearly a tactic of the enemy to derail you from your purpose. When Moses struck the Egyptian slavedriver dead, we can categorize that as a poor choice. While his heart for justice and the displeasure of the mistreatment of his people was in the right place, the way he went about it was not. By killing the Egyptian slavedriver out of anger, he was circumventing God's plan by taking matters into his own hands. He assumed the role of judge, jury, and executioner. He, in essence, took the position of God and, in doing so, found himself fleeing as a fugitive. However, when he surrendered to the will of God and accepted the assignment to rescue the Hebrew people, which was his heart's cry for justice, this time it yielded a more favorable result.

Pharoah served as his adversary to derail him from his purpose. In *Ephesians 6:12*, we're told that our struggle isn't always as is it seems: *"For our struggle is not against flesh and blood, but against the rulers, against the authorities, against the powers of this dark world and against the spiritual forces of evil in the heavenly realms (NIV).* He experienced repeated opposition from Pharaoh to do the will of God. Despite the adversity, he was victorious in his mission. He was no longer taking the role of God, but rather allowing himself to be used by God instead, which yielded better results. Not only did he fulfill a segment of his purpose but also the Hebrew people benefitted, and God received the glory from all the surrounding nations that heard about a God who rescued His people. Let's look at our own lives and take ownership of what's ours to claim and what should be assigned to our adversary, the enemy.

STEPS OF FAITH

- Think back on the challenges you faced. Were the obstacles, setbacks, and challenges, in part, from poor choices or poor planning, or can you attribute this opposition to the enemy?
- Ask the Holy Spirit for discernment, the ability to objectively see your situation for what it is. Through the clear view of your circumstance, you can "rightly" assign it to the enemy or to poor choices.
- Don't be afraid of the silence from God as you wait to hear what God has to say to you. Give the Holy Spirit time to guide you. This reflection and self-awareness aren't designed to be accusatory. If you're experiencing any blame or shame, it's not of God. God's whispers of correction are always lovingly designed to beckon you toward healing and wholeness.
- Be patient with yourself and allow yourself time for this exercise.

We tend to rush through practices such as this one, but we can gain great rewards by sitting with God. Too often, we're grateful for overcoming the challenge without reflecting or debriefing with ourselves. We overlook praising GOD for what He helped us overcome and the fruit it produced. Either way, I invite you to view this as an opportunity for God to do great things through you. *"All things work together for good for those that love the Lord according to His purpose" (Romans 8:28 KJB)*

These types of self-reflection exercises can be emotionally challenging to do. It may seem insignificant in the grand scheme of things. We want to get to the good stuff, the doing of the actionable steps of the things that God has laid on our hearts. We want to produce that project, pursue that lead, make that call, create! After all, we were made to create. If you're anything like me, I was my worst enemy in the sense I often would rush to do and create and skipped reflecting, thinking, planning, and inviting God in the process. I'm a doer, so I would do things without inviting God into the equation and, oftentimes, it didn't bear the fruit I hoped. All the "life happenings" didn't stop me from moving forward. It was me! I stopped myself from moving forward by how I was choosing to handle the obstacles in those unforeseen situations. Don't get me wrong; I experienced success, but, sometimes, I would hit a wall or a plateau when I should have soared. I couldn't sustain the momentum that was possible. I didn't understand why? I thought I wasn't doing something right, but my thought patterns and my way of operating during certain situations became my nemesis. Does any of this resonate with you? If so, then seek to find those weak points, identify their roots, and create a plan that will lead you to experience more of what God is calling you to. I want to be careful not to paint this picture that there won't be obstacles, but when they surface, how can you move past them by being Victorious!

So, put on your seat belt, and let's take this journey together. We're headed someplace great. Ready! Let's Go!

You were made with purpose for a purpose!

KNOW THYSELF:

Let us test and examine our ways,
and return to the Lord!

Lamentations 3:40 ESV

YOUR EARTHLY HISTORY

Shine Bright: Embrace and Uproot the Past

We know that if we don't learn from history, we're doomed to repeat it. George Santayana said, "Those who cannot remember the past are condemned to repeat it." God constantly called the Israelites who were set free from slavery in Egypt to remember the past, not to stay in the past but to remember the past so they could move forward and equip their future descendants with valuable information. *"So Moses told the people, 'Remember this day, the day you came out of Egypt, out of the house of slavery; for the LORD brought you out of it by the strength of His hand...' (Exodus 13:3 BSB).* In fact, they were not only to remember it but also explain and pass these stories to future generations so they could learn from their forefathers' shortcomings and strengths. They could also understand the reasons why things were the way they were and why they were prone to do what they do. We find an example of this further in Chapter 13:

And on that day you are to explain to your son, 'This is because of what the LORD did for me when I came out of Egypt." It shall be a sign for you on your hand and a reminder on your forehead that the Law of the LORD is to be on your lips. For with a mighty hand the LORD brought you out of Egypt. Therefore you shall keep this statute at the appointed time year after year... In the future, when your son asks you, "What does this mean?" you are to tell him, "With a mighty hand the LORD brought us out of Egypt, out of the house of slavery. And when Pharaoh stubbornly refused to let us go, the LORD killed every firstborn in the land of Egypt, both of man and beast. This is why I sacrifice to the LORD the firstborn male of every womb, but I redeem all the firstborn of my sons." So it shall serve as a sign on your hand and a symbol on your forehead, for with a mighty hand the LORD brought us out of Egypt. (Exodus 13: 8-16 BSB)

In the remembering, we can pay homage, reflect, learn about ourselves, respect the journey of those who paved the way before us, and, in some cases, reap healing, wisdom, and greater understanding for ourselves. God desired that they remembered the things their forefathers did that became a stumbling block for them and how He rescued them time after time so they wouldn't doubt His ability to meet their every need. The testimony of our forefathers can be our testimonies for today. The wisdom that can be gained can help us avoid many of the trials and tribulations that didn't serve them well.

Our past can give us some insight on why we think the way we do. Our mental state of being and behavior can be rooted in our past, and we may not be aware. Whether those roots come from good soil or undernourished soil can be the difference between a thriving life experience and one that keeps us stuck, unable to live the abundant life that our God always desired for us to live. We're going to take a journey to learn from our personal history that existed long before we took our first breath, the one we were born into. Why? Because what I've found in my own life and what studies support is that we can embody past traumas in our bodies that aren't ours but passed down to us from generations past. What we've inherited informs and casts a shadow on how we move about the world for better or worse. And, like a cancer, if we don't address it, it can metastasize or wreak havoc in other parts of our body. However, we know that when we're correctly diagnosed, we can set out to take the necessary steps to address the root cause, and a prescription can then be prescribed for healing to be possible.

Similarly, if you're unaware of the amazing contributions of your ancestors, you can be deprived of the part of your identity that makes you unique and special. I remember I was astounded that there were seven influential African empires that had a huge impact on history from the second millennium BC to the 13th century BC. Unfortunately, this history wasn't the history I was taught in school, therefore, depriving me of the great strides my ancestors contributed. I was even more astonished to learn that there was an African prince named Abdul-Rahman ibn Ibrahima Sori who was born in Guinea, West Africa who found himself on a slave ship headed to Natchez, Mississippi. According to Wikipedia, he was made Amir by his father, which meant he was given military command of an army of 2,000 men. He spoke four languages and was a learned man who knew how to read and write. He was given the mission to "protect the African coast and strengthen their economic interests in the region." During this mission, he was taken into captivity by other Africans who then sold him and his surviving men to English slave traders in 1788 in exchange for weapons, and other goods. They brought them from the shores of Africa to America. Upon arrival, "he labored on the cotton plantation of Thomas Foster for more than thirty-eight years before gaining his freedom." And yet, these stories and many more get lost, thereby diminishing the lives that were changed forever. While this isn't my personal story it was good to know that the Africans who were enslaved weren't merely uneducated savages but were a people group that were accomplished in their own right.

STEPS OF FAITH

- I would like you to explore your personal ancestry. Technology and DNA has made it easy to gain some idea of your genetic make-up and story. Were you able to find anything, and, if so, how has this new information informed your present?
- Ask the elders of your family to share their stories. I'm sure they would love to share. You might be surprised with what you find. Their stories are your stories and may shine some light on your own story.

I was invited to a screening of a short film called, Open Wounds. I really didn't have much expectation other than the group I was part of strongly recommended it. I'm glad that I trusted their recommendations because it was an evening well spent. This documentary chronicled the journey of Phil Allen, Jr who sought to deal with the unaddressed wounds that his family experienced as a result of the unsolved racially motivated murder of his grandfather. Phil uncovered the aftermath of the murder of his grandfather, which led subsequently to the healing that occurred for his family after telling the story. Confronting what had happened allowed room for healing to occur within his family. After the screening, we were invited to a panel discussion. During this panel discussion, I learned the scientific term, "epigenetics," which explains the effects of trauma on a family and future generations. Epigenetics is a controversial term among the medical field, but so was PTSD when it was first introduced. Now PTSD is widely acknowledged and accepted in the medical field. I believe epigenetics will have the same acceptance someday. So, what is epigenetics? Epigenetics means that trauma can be passed down from one generation to the next, not in its original form but a version of it. It's believed that trauma from the father may skip the daughter but get passed down to the son or it may skip a generation and emerge in another generation.

According to Martha Henriques's article on March 26, 2019, a 2013 study found an intergenerational effect of trauma associated with scent. According to Henriques,

> The researchers blew acetophenone – which has the scent of cherry blossom – through the cages of adult male mice, zapping their feet with an electric current at the same time. Over several repetitions, the mice associated the smell of cherry blossom with pain. Shortly afterwards, these males bred with

female mice. When their pups smelled the scent of cherry blossom, they became more jumpy and nervous than pups whose fathers hadn't been conditioned to fear it. To rule out that the pups were somehow learning about the smell from their parents, they were raised by unrelated mice who had never smelt cherry blossom. "The grandpups of the traumatised males also showed heightened sensitivity to the scent. Neither of the generations showed a greater sensitivity to smells other than cherry blossom, indicating that the inheritance was specific to that scent. This sensitivity to cherry blossom scent was linked back to epigenetic modifications in their sperm DNA. Chemical markers on their DNA were found on a gene encoding a smell receptor, expressed in the olfactory bulb between the nose and the brain, which is involved in sensing the cherry blossom scent. When the team dissected the pups' brains, they also found there was a greater number of the neurons that detect the cherry blossom scent, compared with control mice.

I'm fascinated by this study, because we know that our environments and situations can induce stress in our bodies that can contribute to our blood pressure and heart conditions. We know those who are at a high risk for heart conditions are told to minimize their stress level. We know stress can have an adverse effect on our mental state. While epigenetics is highly debated. Let's suppose there might be something there that we can use for our benefit.

I sense that the sentiment among some White people in America is one of confusion. They can't fully comprehend why Black people can't move past slavery. They say, "It was hundreds of years ago. There are plenty of successful Black people today. There are more people of color in positions of authority and power than ever before." I sense my White brothers and sisters want Black people to move on and be satisfied with the strides they were allowed to have and put the past behind. However, it goes so much deeper than that. You can't move on until you acknowledge and address the past and make peace with it.

If we look at slavery, it was so atrocious. You uproot a people group unwillingly from their homeland, family, culture, language, and livelihood. You place them in a foreign climate after traveling thousands of miles under the harshest conditions. Then you further strip them of their identity and dignity by shackling them like animals. You separate them from their families, thereby creating generations of men ill-equipped to be husbands and fathers because that was stripped from them. Remember, a child learns how to become a husband, a wife, a parent by what's modeled for them. That natural order of modeling and learning is stolen and not modeled properly for generations, and then you find new ways to imprison Black men and profit from it by creating a system that further victimizes the victim. You make them feel they're to blame for their predicament. They aren't educated enough, but the system was designed not to educate the slaves and then you create school systems again that ensure they get a substandard education to maintain this disparity and further victimization. You label them lazy and criminals and then we as society begin to agree with this assessment and say, "Yeah, they're just lazy and a scourge on society. They're responsible for their predicament. It's no fault but their own." I see generations of men trapped in this cycle. Henceforth, a cycle begins. I have long heard that if you tie the foot of a baby elephant down from moving it will struggle until it believes it can no longer move and when you use that same restraint when the elephant becomes an adult, it will still believe that it's shackled. It won't move. It has the capability to break free due to its sheer power, but now it has been conditioned to believe that it's not free to move.

We want to acknowledge the reality of our past, address it, and make peace with it. We don't want the past to condition us to the point where it has the power to hinder us from living and operating fully in the way God intended us to live. It's said that we're spiritual beings having an earthly experience.

There are also bodies in the heavens and bodies on the earth. The glory of the heavenly bodies is different from the glory of the earthly bodies. The sun has one kind of glory, while the moon and stars each have another kind. And even the stars differ from each other in their glory. It is the same way with the resurrection of the dead. Our earthly bodies are planted in the ground when we die, but they will be raised to live forever. Our bodies are buried in brokenness, but they will be raised in glory. They are buried in weakness, but they will be raised in strength. They are buried as natural human bodies, but they will be raised as spiritual bodies. For just as there are natural bodies, there are also spiritual bodies. (I Corinthians 15: 40-44 NLT)

From the time we take our first breath as a baby, the clock starts the depreciation of our bodies. While our bodies have an expiration date, our Spirit is infinite. We're told we'll have a glorified body when our earthen vessels are no more. We human beings are so complex in the way that we're created. The medical field is still trying to understand our brain and everything that makes us so unique from every other creature on this planet. There are so many factors that contribute to shaping our essence. The time in which we live, our origin, culture, economic status, educational, political, and social realities shape us. It can lead us to our purpose or lead us astray never operating in our unique purpose.

We are going to study our history for several reasons:

1. Know where we came from.
2. Learn from our mistakes.
3. Avoid mistakes from the past.
4. Inform our future.

If you don't learn from your past mistakes or weaknesses that are inherently a part of you; you'll inevitably repeat them again. It's like gravitating to the wrong man and you ask yourself why men are dogs. Well, little grasshopper, all men aren't dogs; you just keep attracting them because you haven't studied your history well. So, you keep doing the same things, wishing and hoping for a different outcome. If you've been around the block, they call that insanity. We don't want to live in insanity; we want to live in the freedom that comes from Jesus our Lord and Savior. This is what God desires for you. Ask the Holy Spirit to guide you this time.

STEPS OF FAITH

- What do you know about your grandparents' or parents' background that may shed some light on your life?

- What's God asking you to surrender from your past to the foot of His cross, so the weight of it won't crush you or everything you touch? Remember, He died to set you free from every bondage.
- What past hurt does He want you to allow Him to heal, so you don't sabotage yourself? *Remember, He died to heal you from all infirmities.
- What are the people closest to you, whom you trust, saying to you that you're unwilling to address or in denial about? If you trust them and believe that they love you, receive what they may be offering to you as a gift to change and mature.

As you revisit the past, I want you to know that *"there is no condemnation for those who belong to Christ Jesus" (Romans 8:1 NLT)*. As you unbury or revisit past experiences or unresolved trauma, I want you to keep that at the forefront of your mind. For some of us, we might be entering into a delicate and dangerous territory, so I'm going to encourage you to be patient with yourself and kind to yourself. If you experience shame and or condemnation, I want you to know that this is NOT of God. Our Holy God reveals things to us to help us, not hinder us. Anything that's contradictory to this great truth is NOT of God. It's the "father of lies" and you must remind yourself of what's true about who God says you are. Search the scriptures to learn what God says about you. Here are a few scriptures to start with if you don't already have scriptures readily available to say to yourself:

The Bible says,

"For we are God's masterpiece. He has created us anew in Christ Jesus, so we can do the good things he planned for us long ago"

(Ephesians 2:10 NLT).

"And may you have the power to understand, as all God's people should, how wide, how long, how high, and how deep his love is"

(Ephesians 3:18 NLT).

"Who shall separate us from the love of Christ? Shall tribulation, or anguish, or persecution, or famine, or nakedness, or peril, or sword?"

(Romans 8:35 ASV).

"You made all the delicate, inner parts of my body and knit me together in my mother's womb"

(Psalm 139:13 NLT).

These are a few scriptures of many that will affirm you and define how God sees you and how you MUST see yourself. Take the time to mine these treasures in the pages of His love letter, the Bible. The Bible is a combination of a love letter, a compass, a manual, and your ancestral history.

STEPS OF FAITH

- Grab an index card and write the scriptures above, so you can commit them to memory. Place them in places where you'll see them frequently so that you immerse yourself in God's truth. You want to recall these truths when you need them most.
- Once you've committed these scriptures to memory, I challenge you to discover other scriptures that will encourage you, edify you, and remind you of God's love for you.

I'm encouraging you to make it a daily practice to memorize scripture because when you find yourself in a tough situation, you want to be able to speak God's truth over yourself at a moment's notice. Once, when I was riddled with anxiety, I found a scripture that spoke to the core of this issue for me. *"Do not be anxious about anything, but in everything with prayer and supplication with thanksgiving give all your requests to God. And the peace of God will guard your heart in Christ Jesus" (Philippians 4:6 KJV)*. I would meditate on it and repeat it to myself until I understood it mentally and believed it in the core of my being. As I meditated on this scripture, God revealed to me that my anxiety was born out of my independence from Him and dependence on myself. If I were solely dependent on me, then it made sense that I was so anxious. I needed to be reminded that I serve a big God who desires for me peace. *"Peace I leave with you, My peace I give to you; not as the world gives do I give to you. Let not your heart be troubled, neither let it be afraid" (John 14:27 NKJV)*. And HE wants to give me the things that concern me and those I love.

Which of you, if your son asks for bread, will give him a stone? Or if he asks for a fish, will give him a snake? If you, then, though you are evil, know how to give good gifts to your children, how much more will your Father in heaven give good gifts to those who ask him!"

(Matthew 7: 9-11NIV)

OR *"Consider the ravens: they neither sow nor reap, they have neither storehouse nor barn, and yet God feeds them. Of how much more value are you than the birds!" (Luke 12:24 ESV)*. Once I reached that place of truly embracing and believing what this scripture said, then the hold the spirit of anxiety had over me dissipated. If you noticed

I called it a "spirit." You can agree or disagree with me by assigning anxiety as a spirit, but God called fear a spirit in *2 Timothy 1: 7 NKJV: "For God has not given us a spirit of fear, but of power and of love and of a sound mind."* As I read this scripture, I can't help to see that fear is referred to as an entity that has energy and is active. God reminds us that He didn't give us this fear, but, instead, He gave us something greater than fear. The tools He gives us to combat fear is *His power, love, and a sound mind.* Anything else, like fear, worry, and anxiety, which I call kissing cousins, aren't from Him but rather from the "father of lies." *"Perfect love cast out all fears" (I John 4:18).* Again, we see just like fear is active, love is active as well. In fact, in this scripture I see love is more powerful because God is love. He made us with love to love. Love has the power to destroy what fear, anxiety, comparison, low self-esteem, lack mindset, procrastination, doubt, and a host of other ways of thinking that tend to create pitfalls, obstacles, and habits that prevent us from flourishing in the way we were designed and created to flourish. Those unexpected situations that are beyond our control, that threaten to curtail our progress, will take different forms. Why do some people rise above them but others succumb and just give up? It starts in the mind. Some have the mental capacity to see past their current situation and forge ahead while others do not. This was one of my struggles. I didn't always struggle with this, but, sometimes, the self-talk

PART III

in my head made it difficult to do the things I wanted to do. During these times, I had to establish a plan to prepare myself for those moments when what was going on internally wasn't serving me well.

I had a season in my life when fear seemed to want to grab me and paralyze me, but God brought me to *1 John 4:18 NLT: "Such love has no fear, because perfect love expels all fear. If we are afraid, it is for fear of punishment, and this shows that we have not fully experienced his perfect love."* God invited me to do two things in that season. First, to look at where I may not be operating in love with myself or in my relationships. Secondly, He was inviting me to accept the fullness of His love that could heal every broken place, every generational hurt, every system designed to hinder, every word designed to be a stumbling block to be cast out by His power and love. This also required me to forgive. Unforgiveness and love can't exist in the same space because if you can't forgive, that means you may be harboring anger and hate, which leaves no room to receive love or give it. He wanted me to choose to bask in His love. *"May you experience the love of Christ, though it is too great to understand fully. Then you will be made complete with all the fullness of life and power that comes from God"* (Ephesians 3:19 NLT). He wanted me to experience what it feels like to be made complete with all the fullness of life and power that comes from God. I wanted to experience that too. I found myself intentionally reprogramming my brain until I could fully embrace truth, until the lies that were spoken to me or I adopted as truth became nonexistent.

Fear, anxiety, and worry, as I mentioned, are like cousins. They feed off one another and none will serve you well. I must say that if you have a medical condition, then disregard what I have to say on this matter. But I'll offer this: our Western culture often is too quick to label and prescribe pharmaceuticals. My kids and I laugh when we listen to some pharmaceutical commercials. The product promises to give you great skin, but you might lose a limb in the process. Who needs a limb? I know I'm overexaggerating, but I'm sure you've heard those commercials with the disclaimer at the end that's either said too fast that the human ear can catch what's said or written so small that you need a magnifying glass to read it. Let's be clear; I'm not opposed to medicine. I've benefited from physicians and medicine and believe God allows man to create medicine to improve the lives of mankind. However, we know that when money enters the picture, any good thing can become corrupt when greed is in the mix.

I remember when I was in college, I was in excruciating pain. The pain was debilitating. I couldn't sit, stand, walk, or urinate without experiencing pain. I thought I was dying. I was advised to go to the chiropractor. I'm so thankful for the person who recommended I do that. I went to this chiropractor, expecting him to make the pain go away, give me some medication, STAT! I needed drugs! Nope, he prescribed no drugs. He said it would only mask the root of the problem. He methodically adjusted my spine for several weeks, and all the symptoms I was experiencing went away. I had a pinch nerve that was the root cause of all the other symptoms I was experiencing. We don't always want to go to the root cause, because that will take too much time. We don't want to invest the time. We want quick results. We want to experience no pain. Unfortunately, quick fixes only mask what's truly going on beneath the surface. I'm thankful he was reluctant to give me pain killers, and I'm glad I trusted him as a physician.

I want us to choose not to mask what's truly going on beneath the surface but unmask the core issues. Why is this important to do? I've found in my life and the lives of those close to me that we already possess power and light. The power and light that resides within us can potentially remain dormant and never come to the surface. Apostle Paul describes power and light in this prayer,

> *I also pray that you will understand the incredible greatness of God's power for us who believe him. This is the same mighty power that raised Christ from the dead and seated him in the place of honor at God's right hand in the heavenly realms.*

(Ephesians 1: 19-20 NLT)

Paul also said, *"The Spirit of God, who raised Jesus from the dead, lives in you. And just as God raised Christ Jesus from the dead, he will give life to your mortal bodies by this same Spirit living within you" (Romans 8: 11 NLT).* We want to uncover and expose anything that might hinder this power and light within us. My heart's desire is that not just a few courageous ones but many will shine brightly for the glory of God. When more and more of God's children shine brightly, we all benefit. God mandates we take dominion over all He has created. We can't take dominion if we're bound by lies we've inherited or allowed to set up shop in our minds. So, let's get to the root cause. Let's be courageous!

STEPS OF FAITH

- Write down every lie you allowed the enemy to convince you as truth, whether it was spoken to you as reality or you said it to yourself.
- Now that you've identified what's not true, I challenge you to find more great truths in the Bible to combat the lies of the enemy. Whenever a lie wants to rear its ugly head, I want you to remind the lie of what's true. Speak the truth often enough and you'll soon forget the lies that once held such great power in your mind.

PART III

Remember, this enemy is opposed to any plan that God has for your life. The enemy was relentless in his opposition to Jesus in the garden. Why? Satan knew that our Almighty God was about to do something in and through Jesus that was going to change all of creation forever. The enemy was relentless in tempting Jesus. The enemy tempted Jesus, so, best believe, he will attempt to do the same to you. I say attempt because while he will try, we must know that he's a defeated foe. He will NEVER be successful unless we give Him the ammunition to be successful. His strategies will take various forms; it may even be subtle. He will use situations, people, circumstances, your past, and even those words that we unknowingly spoke over ourselves to distract us from the plan that God has for us. However, one thing I know is that the enemy is no match for the I AM God, the Alpha and Omega Who is, Who was, and forever shall be. We need to remind ourselves of who God is. If you don't know, search the scriptures. Once you understand and believe that the God that is for you and created you is an All-Powerful and All-Knowing God, this should cause you to operate differently. We should conduct ourselves accordingly because we have the cards stacked in our favor. The British Royal family are clear on their birthright and what that birthright grants them. They know they have unhindered access to the Palace and all the benefits and responsibilities that come with the title and residents of the Palace. We too have the same access and privileges given to us by the King of kings and the Lord of lords. We are joint heirs with Jesus. Take a moment to let that great truth sink in. However, we don't operate as princes and princesses, but rather as abandoned children. We either forget or are clueless to our true identity and the authority given to us by God. Rather we operate as victims rather than victors. As followers of Christ, we celebrate Easter, which I prefer to call Resurrection Sunday, believing we have victory over death and the wiles of the enemy, but we don't always operate like we do. When the celebration is done, we tend to forget the truth and reality of what Jesus did on the cross as One who sits on the throne at the right hand of the Father. We live lives not reflective of the sacrifice and victory.

None of that toxic self-talk is from God, and you must treat those voices as attacks of the enemy, as weapons assigned to destroy you. It's wise to seek Godly counsel and, in some cases, it may be prudent to seek professional counsel to help you navigate and process any trauma that you may not have dealt with. If you're having a tough time with this exercise, be kind to yourself. The purpose of this exercise is to reprogram what the enemy has convinced us as true and replace it with what's actually true about who we are and who we belong to. Now believe it!

PART III

STEPS OF FAITH

- I'm going to challenge you to write your current situation and your history that you've used as excuses, that led to doubt, procrastination, and self-sabotage but served as plausible reasons to delay the things that God has told you to do. You decided to put it to the side, but, at the core, it was rooted in fear, and it was safer to do nothing than to do something.
- Take what you've written down and sit with it. Acknowledge what you've written and put it in its proper place. What you have written will inform you but not take center stage in your life. Devise a plan with God to dethrone these potential pitfalls.

Embrace and Make Peace with the Past

The history we're born into is the one we need to learn and embrace. Embrace ALL of it! The good, the bad, and the ugly. Why? Because whether we realize it or not, we're operating in our present life with the residue of generations past. This can be a good or bad thing. Whatever the history, we want to use all of it because God can use it all. I first heard this saying from a dear friend of mine: God can use all our mess; none of it goes to waste, just like manure. He uses the waste of animals and it's repurposed as fertilizer to grow our food. Only God can orchestrate such a thing. I want you to adopt this mindset that whatever life has handed you, whether it was given to you or a product of your own making, doesn't have to be the end of your story. It's very important because, most likely, what preceded you has shaped you. Your parents raised you from the lens that was handed down to them, that they, in turn, handed to you. Depending on your awareness, you'll knowingly or unknowingly pass it on to your kids, and they'll hand down a version of it to their kids, and so it goes. There are some cycles we want to avoid operating in and pass down to our kids. We need to understand that we can inherit and pass down history that's worthy of passing forward, but others should be uprooted and destroyed.

We can also understand why we're drawn to certain things such as justice, business, art, sports, etc. from knowing ourselves well. As I mentioned, we want to embrace the good, the bad, and the ugly of our history. I'm going to share mine with you. Here is one of many good stories about my history that was passed on to me by my grandmothers. Their zeal for God in their worship and prayer was modeled for me from a young age. I could remember watching my grandmother on my mother's side worshipping God and praising Him out loud with fervor. She loved Jesus with all her being. All her grandbabies would come to her as adults, asking her to pray for them because we all believed she had a direct line to God like no one else had. However, I have learned we all have that same direct line; we just have to fervently seek after it. I have another fond memory of my mother praying over my wedding day. My wedding was supposed to be an outdoor ceremony. Unfortunately, hurricane Bertha had other plans. As I looked out my window, I saw the remnants of hurricane Bertha with our backyard tree toppled to the ground. I could only imagine what the venue we secured looked like. As I passed the main bathroom, I saw my mom staring out of our second-floor bathroom window praying. While I couldn't make out what she was saying, I knew she was praying on behalf of my wedding day. I know she was praying that God would hold the hurricane at bay and prevent it from ruining the day. While we weren't able to hold the ceremony outdoors, the storm did subside, and the sun came out and we were able to take pictures outside after the ceremony. What a great feeling to know that my mom was covering my marriage and my wedding day in prayer. This is my history. This is my inheritance that has shaped my journey, and for that I am grateful.

The Good

As immigrants to the United States, my parents came with the intention to carve out a future that wasn't possible in Haiti. Like many immigrants, they arrived on American soil with the hopes and expectation of economic freedom and opportunity. Therefore, they passed down the same desire and passion to me and my sisters, along with a strong work ethic and a propensity toward entrepreneurship. This is one of the many "good" attributes I inherited from my parents. Although I saw them start small business ventures that gained small victories, their efforts weren't enough to sustain a thriving business. Their desire and dream sparked my own desire to one day start my own business. However, I also bear the reality that they never did experience the success that they wanted to achieve. I often thought I would suffer the same outcome of never reaching the level of success that I knew my parents desired. I quickly realized that their reality didn't have to be mine. I thanked them for planting the seed and being courageous enough to try.

The Bad

One childhood experience that I would attribute as "bad" stemmed from my fourth- and fifth-grade experience. I attended the local public school walking distance from my home in Elizabeth, New Jersey. I experienced bullying from Black students. Somehow, my Caribbean background was offensive. It got so bad that our principal, Ms. Reiley, walked us home. We were taunted about our Haitian background as something that's bad. My self-esteem and identity definitely took a beating. However, during those years, I encountered my teacher, Ms. McClain, whom I loved. She was so much fun. We did so many creative projects and played a game called 7 UP. I suspect she majored in art because I don't remember doing much academic work. I had no idea that she was doing me a disservice. I had no idea what lay ahead in my academic journey, and I paid the price. While she was a fun teacher, I was ill-prepared to be successful academically. After finishing my fifth grade there, I transferred to a private Catholic middle school primarily because of the bullying. I just about failed everything my first semester there. I soon realized what I didn't get in the public school. I struggled with Language Arts. I found myself always having to play catch up in English and math. I never thought I was a great writer because I struggled in this area. Thank goodness I didn't allow this small part of my story to deter me from writing. My editor told me I have above average writing skills. This is another story of victory! What the enemy meant for evil God used for my ultimate good because I allowed God to. Another unexpected gift that emerged from my time at Immaculate Conception brought me to a group of students who shared my same ethnic and cultural background. There, God slowly restored my self-esteem and pride in my Haitian heritage. God met me in those broken places of my story, and He continues to use it for His glory.

The Ugly

As a little girl, a trusted family member violated my innocence. This "ugly" part of my story could have broken me in a million pieces; thankfully, it didn't. I can share my molestation devoid of shame or anger only because of my relationship with God. God slowly restored my voice and self-worth as an adult when I came to terms with what happened to me. My voice was squelched when my perpetrator manipulated me to believe that speaking out would cause my parents to be displeased with me. When I became a mom, my desire to ensure my kids never experienced such a violation in their lifetime was important to me. Thankfully, this trauma didn't break me but, rather, fueled a fire within me to support organizations that work toward restoring women who have been violated or sexually exploited in one way or another. I allow myself to be vulnerable and courageous with my story to encourage others not to hide the brokenness of their story. Exposing the evil positioned me to expose what was done in the dark from wreaking havoc on my mind and spirit. Bringing it to the light prevents me from being held hostage from what wasn't my shame to carry. I pray if this is remotely your story that you'll find a safe place and courage to share your story. I promise that you'll feel lighter as you release this weight that was never yours to carry. The effects of my trauma caused me to address my propensity toward people pleasing and finding my voice. It took years before I could find my authentic voice. That's why it's important to delve into every aspect of our past by gently examining it to see if parts of our stories may be hindering us from being fully who GOD has called us to be. While I would rather not have had that horrible experience, I've learned to embrace and turn what the enemy meant for evil and allow God to use it for good. I've become an advocate for those who don't have a voice today so they can find their voice one day.

That's why I'm excited that a portion of the sale of this book will go to amazing organizations like Dressember and Treasures designed to support and assist females who've been sexually trafficked, forced into the adult sex industry or entered it willingly due to circumstances. Whatever the case, I'm excited that I could be a small part of someone's restoration that, in turn, restores my story.

While it will be hard to revisit these past experiences, it's necessary to embrace them in your timing. For some, you may be visiting these experiences for the first time. If so, I encourage you to be gentle with yourself and give yourself grace. Keep in mind that God can use these traumatic and nontraumatic experiences for His glory. I want to encourage you to use wisdom. You may need to seek professional counseling or a small recovery group to help you process these experiences.

There are great benefits that can be gained in getting counseling and or attending a small recovery group. As I mentioned in an earlier chapter, I felt the prompting of the Holy Spirit to seek some help because I found myself not being able to say, "no" and to set healthy boundaries with those I loved. I soon came to realize that I possessed some co-dependent behavior that stemmed from my childhood. I thrived from being needed. It also gave me some insight as to why I was experiencing stagnation from moving forward fully in my personal life. I didn't realize how my personal story had such an impact on my present until the Lord was bringing these things to my awareness. Everything was affected from raising my kids to my marriage and career. I wanted to break cycles. I wanted to avoid passing faulty tools that served me well during my trauma but wouldn't continue to do so if I wanted to live more in the healing that God desires for me and less in the trauma.

I'm reminded of how generational sins and cycles are nothing new; they're evident in the Book of Genesis. You can see how generational sins continue to the next generation. This generational sin can manifest as a curse. Adam and Eve are great examples of this. We see that God tells Adam and Eve, our ancestors, not to partake of the fruit from the Tree of Good and Evil and the Tree of Life. They can eat from the million other trees He provided for them, just not those two. We, who identify ourselves as Christ-followers, acknowledge that we've inherited this sin nature that was established by Adam and Eve's disobedience. Their disobedience toward GOD's instruction became a sin, thereby severing their close relationship with God, which was free of isolation, death, lack, fear, and shame. As a consequence of their disobedience, they were cursed, and their offspring would also experience the consequences of their disobedience. However, we know we're set free from the curse with Jesus.

I want to offer you some encouragement. You can break the cycles of sin. I find an example of this in Isaac's, Jacob's, and Joseph's stories where we see how favoritism, jealousy, manipulation, and deceit gets repeated in this family's history. We find Isaac and Rebecca, parents of twins Esau and Jacob, demonstrate their favoritism toward their children. As a parent my sons always ask me, "Mom, am I your favorite?" And I respond with, "Yes!" I always tell each of them they're my favorite. I love them equally for different reasons. They would say their sister is my favorite, but again I'll say they're all my favorites. I won't fall into that trap! I never wanted to foster an environment where any of my kids would be jealous of one another. So, in scriptures, Rebecca clearly had a favorite in Jacob and helped Jacob deceive his father to steal his older brother's inheritance. What mom does that!? This ignited hatred between the brothers, which caused Jacob to flee because his brother wanted to kill him. Fast forward, Jacob desired to wed Rachel but was deceived by her father who caused

Jacob to wed her older sister Leah. Nothing good comes from deception and manipulation! Jacob who manipulated and deceived his father and brother finds himself on the receiving end as Rachel's father uses manipulation and deception on Jacob when he agrees to work for his father-in-law to wed Rachel his true love. Ultimately, he's wed to both sisters, and we find their offspring develop a jealousy for Joseph, the younger brother, the product of Jacob and Rachel, his first love, and Jacob's favorite of all his sons. We see history repeating. This all sets up a recipe for disaster! Then the plot thickens as the brothers devise a plan to kill Joseph, the favored younger brother, and would have, except their younger brother, Benjamin, intercede and convince them to sell Joseph instead. We see how jealousy, deception, manipulation, and the need to control plagues this family's ancestry.

It's interesting to see that this family's history of deception and manipulation caused separation. Adam and Eve's manipulation and deception by the snake caused their separation from God. Jacob's manipulation and deception to his brother causes him to flee and be separated from his family. Finally, Joseph's brothers' deception and manipulation caused Joseph to be separated from his loved ones. In each instance, we see a separation and unaddressed cycles that can occur in a family. However, we see Joseph breaking this cycle by using deception and manipulation but only to search the hearts of his brothers, which led to forgiveness, thereby reconciling with his brothers and unifying the family once again. Joseph's decision to break the cycle preserved a whole people group. As you can see, when one chooses to break a cycle, it can bring about a healing and a blessing for all parties involved, thereby blessing generations to come. I challenge you to look at the issues that plague your family or ancestors. What is it for your family? Manipulation, alcoholism, poverty, promiscuity, low self-esteem, fatherless homes, domestic abuse, food addictions, laziness, etc. Be honest with your history! We want to allow God to break cycles.

STEPS OF FAITH

- Are there any generational cycles that you're aware of? What seems to show up in your family as recurring cycles? Write them down. We want to identify and name them.
- I also challenge you to look for the ones that aren't so blaring as the ones mentioned above. They may be subtle, such as controlling, judging, placing unrealistic expectations, etc.

Now that we've identified the cycles that existed in generations past, our family, and present circumstances, I want you now to take a moment to write down how these things made you feel. Did you feel embarrassed, alone, unaffected, determined to take a different path, aloof, anxious, abandoned, etc.? Give a name to the way these things made you feel. Name these feelings it may give you a window into how you're showing up in your relationships be it personal or professional. It also may give you a window into how you're operating in the world around you; knowingly or unknowingly.

STEPS OF FAITH

- After you name the cycles you're aware of from your grandparents, parents, siblings, aunts, uncles, and cousins, look to see how these cycles affected you one way or another. Write it down.

We can't help but experience the effects of the beliefs, traditions, and circumstances we were born into that shape our perspective. However, all of it proves useful if you choose to see it that way. Lessons available to learn in every challenging experience. I stumbled upon a show called, "Anne with an E," which captured my attention after the first episode. We're taken on this journey of a girl who became orphaned as a baby when both her parents fell ill in the early 1900s. At the age of thirteen, she was adopted by two unmarried siblings, the Cuthberts, a man and a woman past child-bearing age. Their initial introduction to one another isn't pleasant. The adult siblings were under the impression they were adopting a teen boy to help them with the farm, since they were getting up in age. The woman doesn't hide her disappointment and expresses her desire to return Anne to the orphanage. You can imagine that this situation brought about a barrage of disappointments and insecurities for Anne. Her excitement of finally being chosen and finally having a home quickly turned to hurt and pain when she learned the Cuthberts were disappointed and didn't want her. Her insecurities of abandonment and inadequacies erupted to the surface. Eventually, the Cuthberts decide to keep her and pour into her life rather than what they initially desired, which was to get a boy to help with the farm. During the series, we see flashbacks of Anne's experiences as an orphan that were horrifying. We see Anne persevere even when her fellow classmates chide her about being an orphan. They even called her trash. She could have been crushed by the circumstances surrounding her birth, but she didn't allow it to keep her from her dream, hope, and aspiration. Although she persevered, we also see how she was prone to be triggered by her past and how it had the potential to derail her.

We want to make sure the circumstances of our lives don't contain the power to derail us from our purpose to accomplish on this earth. It won't steal our purpose. Instead, we want these circumstances to inform us in a way that spotlights redemption and restoration as a reality.

I'm here to tell you that your past doesn't have to define you. You can only be defined by what you allow. Will it be easy? Of course, it won't be. You're bombarded with so much messaging that can trigger the lies that were deposited into your spirit from long ago. These triggers can seem to affirm what was told to you or imposed on you as true to be accepted as true. You must make a conscious decision to eradicate every thought process that threatens to render you paralyzed and ineffective.

The circumstances of our lives can illuminate our strengths and weaknesses. Our strengths and weaknesses are good to know. We can't address what needs to be addressed if we're unaware. Once we have an awareness, we have the power to make choices in light of what we know. For instance, if we know we have a generational history or propensity toward alcoholism within our family, maybe we want to make the conscious choice to avoid alcohol. However, for other families, that may not be their cross to bear. If poverty seems to be your inheritance, you may want to investigate and explore where this lack mindset stems from.

STEPS OF FAITH

- Where does any form of scarcity or impossibility play out in your history?
- Where have you adopted this way of thinking in your own life?

PART III

Allow Your Strengths to Emerge

Several years ago, I was part of a leadership group, and our assignment was to take a strengths test, which would illuminate our strengths. To be honest, I didn't understand the significance and how it could be useful. Nonetheless, I completed the assignment. Years later, I revisited my results and was astonished at how accurate the test's description was of me. It finally clicked why it was important to do and how I could use it strategically in business and even forming working relationships. I was somewhat familiar with my strengths and weaknesses but didn't realize how these characteristics and attributes were unique to me. This newfound awareness helped me to capitalize on and better develop my strengths. The philosophy behind the strengths test is that it's better to focus on improving your strengths rather than focus your time and attention on your weaknesses, which we often do. I've since adopted this philosophy. Why try to develop an area that will never be our strong suit. Could our time, energy, and resources be better served, focusing on our strengths? I think so! As I study successful people, they seem to know what they do really well and "stay in their lane." What they do well is identify their deficiencies and align themselves with those that meet where they're lacking. They surround themselves with people who are masterful at what they do well. I'm sure you've heard this saying:

"jack of all trades, master of none." We don't want to embody this saying. For me, this is a saying that I can become trapped. One of my strengths is what's termed, Learner. I love to learn, which is a great thing, but I must remind myself that learning isn't enough if I don't implement what I learn and impact others by what I learn. This is how knowing yourself well can be useful.

Earlier, I briefly shared the good, the bad, and the ugly part of my story. These experiences weren't things I inherited. They're unique aspects of my story that contributed to the way I perceive the world and shaped my thoughts about myself. The whole purpose and importance of examining our ancestral history as well as our lived experience is so we can get to a place where our experiences that lead to our thought life don't hinder us from living the abundant life that God says He desires for us. I believe, in many cases, our purposes never fully get realized because of our thought life. Once we get over that hurdle, God can do amazing things with our lives. I love the encounter Jesus had with this man near the pool of Bethesda in John 5:1-17. This lame man had been ill for thirty-eight years. Jesus asked the lame man if he wants to be healed? Why would He ask such a question? Who wouldn't want to get healed? However, I've found that's not always true. We say we want healing, but our actions say otherwise. Change requires effort. The desire to be healed and the commitment to be healed aren't always congruent. The lame man responds to Jesus' question with a yes. Then Jesus instructs him by saying, "Stand up, pick up your mat, and walk!" Jesus didn't touch him or help him up but required him to believe enough to take ownership in his healing. Once the lame man did just as Jesus instructed him to do, he was instantly healed. We say we want healing, but we need to have the faith and the relentless desire to seek after the healing our God so desperately wants to give. A good portion of Jesus' ministry was healing bodies from infirmities, restoring the brokenness of His children, shifting their hearts to repentance, and giving them new eyes to see. As He healed, He didn't impose His prescription for what ails; He waited until people called on Him. He waits until we empty ourselves of self-sufficiency. *"For whoever wants to save their life will lose it, but whoever loses their life for me will find it" (Matthew 16:25 NAS).* There's no way we can save ourselves; when we try, we'll fail miserably. Although, whoever surrenders the reins of their life will then experience true healing. God waits for us to invite Him to heal us. The healing that's possible requires partnership. We must believe that the healing is unequivocally possible, which demonstrates our unwavering faith in who He is and what He can do. We see in Matthew the woman who had an issue of bleeding for twelve years who sought healing in every possible way until she realized her best and only option for healing was to seek after Jesus. So, she risked ridicule and embarrassment.

I can only imagine the smell that must have been emanating from her body, which, most likely, made her unpleasant to be around. However, she wouldn't be dismayed. She was relentless. She was unwavering in her faith that she didn't need a word from Jesus or even a touch but acknowledged that simply touching His garment would heal her *"for she was saying to herself, 'If I only touch His garment, I will get well.' But Jesus turning and seeing her said, 'Daughter, take courage; your faith has made you well.' At once, the woman was made well."* (Matthew 9:21-22 NAS)

It's said that you get a sense of what you're made of when you're under pressure. Since we've taken an exhaustive look at our past. We want to become more aware of our strengths, passions, gifts, and talents. Take some time to celebrate what you've been able to face, embrace, and make peace with.

STEPS OF FAITH

- Find a quiet place to take inventory of what you believe your strengths are.
- Ask trusted family, friends, colleagues what they believe your strengths are?
- Go online to find a strengths test. There may be a cost associated. Consider taking a personality test as well. The more you know yourself and embrace every aspect of yourself the better.

PART IV

KNOW THYSELF:

Trust in the Lord with all your heart, and do not lean on your own understanding. In all your ways acknowledge him, and he will make straight your paths. Be not wise in your own eyes; fear the Lord, and turn away from evil. It will be healing to your flesh and refreshment to your bones.

Proverbs 3:5-8 ESV

YOUR SPIRITUAL HISTORY

You have already been grafted into a story!

You may be thinking. Why was it necessary to unearth all the pain and revisit our story? Well, I hope you were able to see how these things that may seem to be dormant, unaddressed, and seemingly packed away actually have had center stage in your life. These unaddressed hurts can become a Svengali in our lives, causing us to be puppets to a Puppet Master. The Puppet Master in our lives could be hate, unforgiveness, comparison, fear, envy, low self-esteem, unworthiness, abandonment, among a host of other states of being. These unhelpful states rob us of the fruitfulness that God desires for us. I don't know what the past left you to hold as your primary story and identity. I'm here to tell you that our God is inviting you to cut the cords to that which we've allowed the Puppet Master to use to direct and guide our lives. Instead, your Creator wants you to be tethered to Him. Hopefully, the series of questions and guided moments of reflection offered thus far have challenged you to look and investigate the things that have hindered you from wholeness in order to make peace with the past and embrace the past for what it can teach and receive the available freedom. We've focused on our earthly history that we inherited from our family of origin. Now, we're going to spend some focused time on our spiritual history. This spiritual history has the power to help us understand the flaw in our humanity but offer hope in the transformation that's possible when you allow the power of the Holy Spirit to do what it was intended to do. May we come to a place of surrender and grab hold of the truth of our identity given to us by God.

Our God is love. He created His creation out of love to love! *"Most important of all, continue to show deep love for each other, for love covers a multitude of sins" (1 Peter 4:8 NLT).* Therefore, it's necessary for us to receive the love He desires to lavish on us, so that we can then love ourselves fully, so that we can love those placed in our sphere of influence. In accepting the fullness of His love, we can express authentically who we've been created to be and do without apology.

In *Ephesians,* Paul prayed this prayer that's born out of God's heart for us and is my prayer for us.

> *When I think of all this, I fall to my knees and pray to the Father, the Creator of everything in heaven and on earth. I pray that from his glorious, unlimited resources he will empower you with inner strength through his Spirit. Then*

PART IV

Christ will make his home in your hearts as you trust in him. Your roots will grow down into God's love and keep you strong. And may you have the power to understand, as all God's people should, how wide, how long, how high, and how deep his love is. May you experience the love of Christ, though it is too great to understand fully. Then you will be made complete with all the fullness of life and power that comes from God. Now all glory to God, who is able, through his mighty power at work within us, to accomplish infinitely more than we might ask or think. Glory to him in the church and in Christ Jesus through all generations forever and ever! Amen.

(Ephesians 3:14-21 NLT)

Let's take a moment to unpack this passage of scripture. I sense it has a lot to offer us as we understand that we're created lovingly from the God of Love. Once we receive the fullness of His love, we then can claim more of who we were created to be before this world's sin left its mark on us. It's good to revisit our past and put it in its proper perspective, for it's not intended for us to stay there, nor should it be our starting point. Our starting point needs to be God's original intent, which, in John 10:10, is to give us life and give it to us more abundantly. We want to operate *"from his glorious, unlimited resources he will empower you with inner strength through his Spirit"* (Ephesians 3:16 NLT).

What does that mean!? It sure sounds good, and I want more of it. We want to operate from His resources that are glorious and unlimited. What makes it glorious, deserving honor and high praise? According to Wikipedia, "glory" (from the Latin word *Gloria*, 'fame, renown') is used to describe the manifestation of God's presence as perceived by humans according to the Abrahamic religions where God is regarded as the most glorious being in existence and it's considered that human beings are created in the Image of God and can share or participate, imperfectly, in divine glory as image-bearers." Thus, Christians are instructed to "let your light shine before men, that they may see your good works, and glorify your Father in heaven" (Matthew 5:16 BSB) His glorious and unlimited resources is God himself. He will empower us with inner strength through His Spirit.

You got to sit with that verse for a moment. Too often, we read scripture without fully digesting all that it has to offer. I can give you my interpretation of this verse. However, I want you to ask the Holy Spirit what He wants you to gain from this passage designed to empower you and strengthen you from His Spirit. God doesn't want you to stop there. He wants to not only empower you with inner strength from His Spirit but also make your heart His home if you let Him. The only way that's possible is when you trust Him. As you trust Him, your love for God and His love for you will grow strong and deep. May this deep abiding love in Him give us some insight into the depth and breadth of His love for us. Hopefully, we're experiencing that love that's nothing like a familial or romantic love; it's more significant than that. It's love that we won't fully comprehend because there's nothing like His love that we can quite compare. This love from our Creator God will make us whole and full of life; anything else will disappoint us. That promotion, that shiny object, that car, educational degree, or desired relationship can never fulfill the love we were made to receive from God. Now all the honor and praise belong to God, who has the power and desire to do the healing, equipping, empowering, and so much more than our mind can fathom to accomplish His perfect plan in us. Let's praise Him for who He is and what He desires to do. All we have to do is receive His love and accept Him into our hearts. Why wouldn't we want to receive Him into our hearts? Yet, we don't! We push Him away. The gifts He longs to give us are available to us if only we would allow Him to give them.

I want to formally invite you to this Love that God wants to pour over you lavishly. Suppose you've never allowed or accepted Jesus into your heart. I want to extend that invitation to you now. You simply have to acknowledge that you're lost without Him and dead in your sin. Acknowledge you need God, and He demonstrated His love for you by sending His son Jesus to sacrifice His life on the cross so that the sin of death can be defeated, and we can be reconciled to God. Lastly, surrender your life to Him, demonstrate your trust in Him, and allow Him access into your heart. It's that simple! You're now His child, His friend, a joint heir with Jesus meaning that Jesus' inheritance belongs to you as well. Please share with me, a friend, or a pastor that you have taken this monumental step of faith.

Next, you want to grab a Bible or get one so you can begin to read this love letter that describes a God who is zealous for you, who loves you so much that he would go to great lengths to pursue you. You mean that much to Him! I'm excited for you! This journey will have highs and lows, but you'll never regret taking this journey of faith. Don't take this journey alone. Ask God to help you find a community of hungering individuals after God's heart where you can grow, but not a religion. Religion says you have to work to earn God's approval. I'm inviting you into a relationship with Jesus not a religion. Religion says do the right things and God will be pleased with you. Religion seeks to change the outside while the inside is never transformed. Being in a relationship says come as you are, and I'll transform you to wholeness. Your yes is all that God needs from you. He will do the rest. Your intimate times in His word, prayer, praise, and worship will cause a transformation from the inside out. My prayer is that you find a safe place to wrestle, embrace, and ponder God's Word where nothing is added or removed from His, God-breathed, sacred scriptures. As you look for a community, ask God to lead you to where you'll get fed spiritual food. He will show you where. Trust me; He will answer prayers such as that one. He desires you to know Him intimately as He knows you intimately already.

I want you to mine God's Words for His truth about who you are like a miner mines for precious stones embedded in the earth's crevice. You'll find a God who further demonstrates His love by sending us the Comforter, Holy Spirit, to be with us always.

To all who believe in God, we've been given the gift of the Holy Spirit who dwells inside us. Say what now!? Yes, we have the third person of the Godhead dwelling inside us, which means we're never alone. We have a 24-hour comforter, counselor, teacher, guide, and so much more waiting to direct our steps when we need it. That's mind-blowing! Wrap your head around this great truth. The same power that resurrected Jesus is the same power that resides in you. Mind-blowing, I know! When we embrace this great truth and live in this great truth, how can we doubt? How can we live in a lack mindset when we have this infinite power dwelling inside of us? As Christians, we tend to live less like we're victorious and more like we're defeated. We allow what we see to take precedent over the God we can't see. I have to admit that I'm a visual learner. I'm very much affected visually. It became necessary for me to recite scriptures that helped remind me that I serve a mighty

God who's not bound to earthly limitations. Recite this until you believe what you're saying with every fiber of your being: *"If God is for us, who can ever be against us?" Romans 8:31 NLT)* No matter what the enemy wants to hurl at me, I need to stand firm, knowing that the Holy Spirit who dwells in me is greater than my present situation may want to convince me is the end of my story. *"Greater is He that is in me than he that is in the world" (1 John 4:4 NLT).* Therefore, I remind myself with this scripture, *"I will not rely on what I see because I know he is working in the unseen world" (2 Corinthians 4:18).* These are a sample of many scriptures that I commit to memory to speak over myself and remind me of what's true when what I see wants to supersede God's great truths. I encourage you to find scriptures that you can use to recenter yourself when it feels like you're a defeated foe rather than the redeemed child of the Most High God made to live victoriously. When I say, "to live victoriously," I'm not describing a life devoid of turmoil or strife, but a life lived victoriously and abundantly despite life's setbacks and unpredictability.

Our eyes, with the best intentions, can deceive us of the mystery of God. Let's talk about the Holy Spirit! Often, it's the part of the Triune God that's least understood and the person of God that's forgotten or least talked about. Yet, it's the One we're told resides in us once we accept Jesus into our lives. In my childhood in Catholicism, I was taught how to do the sign of the cross. As I obediently did the sign of the cross over my face, I first tapped my forehead with my index finger, then a tap to my heart, followed by a tap to my left heart then the right of my heart saying, "In the name of the Father, Son, and the Holy Spirit, Amen." If I'm honest, I didn't know why I was doing that, and I had a vague understanding of the Triune God or the Trinity, if you will. I somehow missed and dismissed the significance of the Holy Spirit and the power of the Holy Spirit that promises to teach, guide, pray for us, and so much more. When I first read that the same power that resurrected Jesus is the same power that resides in me, I was astonished. *"The Spirit of God, who raised Jesus from the dead, lives in you..." (Romans 8: 11 NLT)* That blew my mind. Let's sit with that scriptural gem given to us. Let's sit with that great truth. Let's chew on it. I imagine the power that it took to resurrect Jesus is so powerful that our earthly minds can't comprehend its meaning, yet we're told this power resides in us. It's mentioned so nonchalantly that you can almost miss this great truth about what's inside you. What's sad is that too many of us, Christ-followers, don't tap into this power that's hidden within us and remains dormant. It wasn't meant to remain dormant. Why would God give us a gift that He didn't intend for us to access for our benefit and His glory? It would be like purchasing a gift for someone you love only to find out they either didn't use it or, worse, gave it to somebody else without opening it first.

Like a diamond, it only becomes a diamond when it can display its brilliance once it has withstood the pressure that caused it to sparkle. Up until that point, it's a dull rock.

Well, my beloved. Our God wants us to sparkle and not remain a dull rock. In fact, when we sparkle, He sparkles even brighter among mankind. He wants to empower us so we can speak and move boldly for His name's sake. When we walk boldly for His glory, we experience the blessings and victory as byproducts of obedience.

As a believer, once you know who you are through the eyes of the One who created you and knitted you in your mother's womb, you're better able to overcome the obstacles that you'll encounter in your life and in your God pursuits. It bears repeating because I've seen too many disenchanted with God because they believed God would now give them the perfect life that simply won't exist while on earth. I'm sorry to be the bearer of this truth; you won't have a life devoid of conflict, trauma, or turmoil. In fact, as I mentioned, the attack from the evil one will probably intensify and take many forms because the enemy of God doesn't want you to glorify God with your life. He wants you to remain stuck in unforgiveness, bitterness, and resentment, and distracted with meaningless tasks that will bear no fruit. So, how does one bear fruit? Well, there are no shortcuts to this process. The only way I know how to gain this insight is by sifting through the bible, His love letter, the manual, the ultimate compass that can encourage you when you don't know where to turn. When I felt like an alien in a foreign land, and the world sought to shake my confidence and doubt the undeniable greatness that resides within me, God's Word re-centered me. It felt uncomfortable to think that greatness resides in me, let alone say it out loud. I thought, *Who am I to say such a thing?* You think that person is full of him or herself. They may seem egoistical. Yet, God calls us His masterpiece. We are made in the image of the Triune God. Again, sit with that great truth. The "US" mentioned when God created the earth in Genesis, which said, *"let us make mankind in our image" (Genesis 1:26 NIV)"* includes God the Father, God the Son, and God the Holy Spirit. We are created in their likeness!

Believe me; if you're earnest in realizing this God-sized pursuit that God has deposited into your heart, people will look at you like an alien. In those moments, when no one understands or can conceive your God vision, you must remain firm and steadfast, knowing if God deposited this desire in your heart, He will fortify you for the journey. You want the power of the Holy Spirit to display the extraordinary in the ordinary. Remember, many thought Noah was foolish to build an ark as he was directed to do by God. They thought he was crazy, but I'm sure when they were drowning, he didn't seem so foolish after all.

I'm comforted by the history that I've inherited from the God who created me because it supersedes all other history's that we've been given that are beautifully flawed from our earthly experience. Why? Because this one offers freedom, redemption, and glorification. We want to see our story through the lens of God's love for us and how He created us. Then we can see the wonderful tapestry of our lives as a redemptive story rather than a tragedy.

The Japanese have this beautiful art form called Kintsugi, in which they take a clay bowl or vase that's broken into pieces and restore it by reassembling the broken parts with gold. Instead of discarding the object by deeming it useless, they manage to repair its flaws. Therefore, they embrace the imperfections and reimagine the object as something so much more beautiful than its original form, than one ever thought could be possible. I love that! Our God wants to do that on a grander scale. He wants to take our broken stories and create something so much more spectacular than you or I could have ever imagined. He is our God, THE ONE who takes *"what the enemy meant for evil and uses it for our good" (Genesis 50: 20)* and is thereby magnified.

I want to encourage you to trust this spiritual history; the truth about your essence and real purpose rather than the one the world will convince you is your purpose.

Let's look at Moses. His heart for justice and, more specifically, justice for his people, the Israelites, was apparent long before God encountered him at the burning bush. When Moses went out amongst his Hebrew people, their suffering and hardship moved his heart. His desire to correct the two Hebrews who were fighting toward reconciliation further demonstrates his passion. His propensity toward justice and reconciliation made him a perfect candidate to lead the Israelites out of Egypt. He had a unique understanding and insight into the palace's inner workings because he was brought up as one of them but fully aware of his ancestral heritage. Moses had no idea his unique story had already positioned him for the ultimate purpose that God would reveal to him at the age of eighty.

STEPS OF FAITH

- Grab a pen and write what you think your purpose calling is.

This calling is what your heart cries out to do before you take your last breath. It may even be something that is a burden in your heart. For instance, the heart for justice, the poor, the illiterate, the imprisoned, the falsely incarcerated, the entertainment industry, mental wellness, racial reconciliation, media, sports, children, foster children, the elderly, etc. These passions can be clues that point you to your purpose. Hopefully, these examples stir up moments when you've experienced compassion or passion that may indicate a calling that's not only to benefit you but others as well, which will then glorify God. It may even be a unique gift that God has given you and you want to honor Him with that gift. Whatever you think it may be, ask God to make it clear to you.

You're made with purpose for a purpose!

PART V

ALL WILL BENEFIT:

As each has received a gift, use it to serve one another, as good stewards of God's varied grace: whoever speaks, as one who speaks oracles of God; whoever serves, as one who serves by the strength that God supplies- in order that in everything God may be glorified through Jesus Christ. To him belong glory and dominion forever and ever. Amen.

1 Peter 4:10-11 ESV

BRING YOUR GIFTS TO THE ALTAR

History: Our Story that's not our own, but to reflect God's glory and worship HIM in all His Glory

Bring your gifts to the altar! The gifts I'm referring to are the gifts that God has given to you as your special portion here on earth as your blessing to be a blessing. The gifts you have been blessed with, such as your talents, abilities, and personality, can be offered up as a sacrifice to God as a sweet-smelling aroma. The blessing can then be reaped by those who are on the receiving end but, most importantly, you bless God with the very gift He gave you.

In the book of Leviticus, Moses was given clear instructions that he was to share with the Israelites the proper procedure to offer a sacrifice to God. The individual, priest, or group had to adhere to strict guidelines to bring the offering, at which time, Aaron and Aaron sons who were chosen as priests were the only ones who could offer these sacrifices to God on the altar on behalf of the one offering it. There were several types of offerings required to atone for sin or an offering of thanks.

However, I want to focus on the offering given as a gift, a tribute to our God as worship of thankfulness. In Genesis, we see that Cain was a farmer and Abel was a shepherd. They both presented their gifts from the work of their hands, their talents, and abilities. Abel's offering was pleasing to the Lord, but Cain's was not.

> *In the course of time Cain brought some of the fruits of the soil as an offering to the Lord. And Abel also brought an offering—fat portions from some of the firstborn of his flock. The Lord looked with favor on Abel and his offering, but on Cain and his offering he did not look with favor.*
>
> (Genesis 4:3-5 NIV)

As I take a closer look at this passage of scripture to discover what made Cain's gift displeasing in God's sight. I see Cain brought "some of his fruits." In contrast, Abel brought the best of the firstborn of his flock. Abel brought the best of his gifts from the works of his hands. While Cain gave some of his fruits, which leads me to believe it wasn't his choice of fruits that displeased God; rather, he gave God something, but not his best. Whatever we give God we want to give our best. Do not mistake this for perfection. He isn't looking for perfection because perfection relies on your ability, but giving your best means you're not withholding anything from Him.

God's Word said that He has already prepared a work for us to do in advance. What?! Another mind-blowing moment. God, You have already prepared a work uniquely designed for me to complete?! That explains everything. It explains the question that many of us are seeking: What's my purpose? What's my calling? Why am I here? or in a mid-life crisis feeling unfulfilled or lost. Some of us don't want to take our last breath with regret. I personally don't want to leave this earth without accomplishing the work that God has prepared for me to do in advance. I hope you feel the same way as well. I suspect that you're experiencing comparable feelings; otherwise, this book wouldn't have piqued your interest or compelled you to get it.

It's interesting how we're obsessed with our purpose. When kids are still forming sentences at the age of three, we ask kids what they want to be when they grow up. Ironically, we ask kids this profound question while we, as adults, still have no clue. Parents are already shaping what their children are going to be in utero by buying that football, that stethoscope, or those ballerina slippers. I suspect it's because we're given an innate knowing that we were uniquely created with a purpose. That, my friends, has been implanted in our hearts before we were formed in our mother's womb. I'm convinced that's why some of us may feel unfulfilled, depressed, or even restless because that longing is implanted in us, which often doesn't become fully realized. So, we chase after what we think is our calling with the wrong motives. We chase after a purpose because of the money it offers, but we're miserable. We chase after a purpose that will make us feel important. Or we chase after a purpose that was mapped out for us by our family, who we are unwilling to disappoint. In Chapter 2 of Genesis, we see that Adam was given a clear purpose. *"The Lord God placed the man in the Garden of Eden to tend and watch over it" (Genesis 2:15 NLT)*. Adam was given an important and necessary assignment. We want to refocus our attention from what WE want to be or what our family or culture says, to what God wants us to do. What was our Potter's intention when He was creating us with such detail? After all, He created us with such intentionality and specificity. We know this because the first two chapters of Genesis demonstrate that He is intentional, detailed, and there's no lack in how He creates us and creation. He created human beings with great pleasure. Lacking nothing! Perfectly made! Utterly pleased! How does that make you feel, knowing you were made lacking nothing? Everything about how you're made is devoid of imperfection. I hope it causes you to walk a few inches taller, not in an obnoxious or arrogant way, but with healthy confidence and certainty that defies anything that you may have had spoken over your life or had spoken over you for whatever reason. May the truth of *"I am fearfully and wonderfully made" (Psalm 139:14 NIV)* rekindle the fire that's within you.

You may take issue with my statement that everything about how you were made is devoid of imperfection, especially if you were born with a physical, mental, emotional, or social disability. But, yes, you are perfectly and wonderfully made. I know it may be hard to wrap your head around the fact that you're perfectly made when what you see doesn't line up with that statement. Our society equates perfection and success differently than God does. God calls you His masterpiece. He doesn't have a caveat that if you have missing limbs or are autistic or impaired, then I can't call you my masterpiece or love you fully.

If you recall, I likened the Kintsugi art form to how God masterfully takes our brokenness and seeming imperfections and transforms us into this wonderful masterpiece. When He calls you His masterpiece, He's not clueless to the obstacles you may face or the deficit in which you must operate from. He knows all those things and still calls you His masterpiece. God is concerned with the heart, the part of us that's not easily seen but is so much more important than the outward appearances that we tend to give more focus and more importance to. You may say, "Sure that's easy for you to say; you're not in a wheelchair for the rest of your life. You're not blind, you're not deaf, you're not _____. I'm sure you can fill in the blank, and you would be right. You may have impairments that are harder to see but that can become crippling like the internal dialogue that prevent you from the very purpose you were created for, like a disorder that society may judge less than perfect or inferior or you yourself view as something that shouldn't be embraced. I still say that you are wonderfully and perfectly made. This scripture does not only apply to us having full presence of mind or all ten toes and ten fingers, but to those who were born too short, too tall, blind, without a limb or two. All were made perfect, devoid of blemish. Your life is not less valuable or less purposeful; in fact, your life may hold greater purpose than those who seemingly have everything yet feel lacking. Nick Vujicic and Joni Eareckson Tada are two individuals who inspire me. They truly embody what it looks like to allow their lives to be used by God to glorify Him, despite their limitations, to benefit others, and as a byproduct of their obedience, they reap the fruit. God isn't interested in what you can do on your own but, rather, what you're willing to allow Him to do through you.

Nick was born without arms and legs at birth and Joni became a paraplegic at the age of 17. We tend to look at outward appearances and I'm guilty of the same. My eyes will trip me up if I am not careful. At first sight, I'm sure Nick Vujicic's peers, who used to mock him and torment him, never imagined that he would one day be recognized as a powerful preacher and international speaker motivating the masses and preaching the gospel. God has a way of choosing "the foolish things of the world to shame the wise; God chose the weak things of the world to shame the strong" 1 Corinthians 1:27 (NIV). In our eyes, he's the least likely, but in God's eyes, he's just the perfect person to motivate the masses and draw them unto Himself. After learning his story, I thought to myself, *If he can do all that at a deficit, then I have no room for excuses.*

Joni Eareckson Tada is another person who has experienced a tragedy. She became a quadriplegic after diving headfirst into the shallow part of the water. That day forever changed her life with the desire to end her suffering; she knew she had to draw on God's strength in order to keep living. She said she asked God

to show her how to live with her new reality. God revealed to her how He wanted to use this tragedy for something good. And that He did! She is the founder of Joni and Friends that helps disabled individuals all around the world with the necessary resources to thrive with the good news of Jesus.

STEPS OF FAITH

- Embrace and celebrate that you're God's masterpiece with all of your flaws or sordid past. Write a prayer of thanksgiving, utilizing 1 Thessalonians 5: 16-18 as your inspiration.
- If you still have a hard time believing you're a masterpiece, that's okay? Allow yourself to be

angry with God and even grieve the loss that comes from your outward limitation; God can handle it. Write it down, then bring it to God and ask Him to transform it to something more phenomenal that you couldn't envision for yourself. Be patient with yourself because God is patient.

Now that we've established that everything about how you were made is good. Let's look at how God has made you different so all of creation can benefit. I'm always relieved that others have passions that are different from mine, especially when it's necessary for the edification of society. I'm thankful some are concerned about issues that I care about but aren't at the top of my list. I'm glad some are passionate about agriculture and love to grow food because I like to eat. While I love the idea of a garden where I can pick fresh fruits and vegetables for my meal, who am I kidding!? I know myself well enough to know that I don't have the temperament for it in my current lifestyle. Gardening requires time, care, commitment, and passion, which I prefer to dedicate to other things. While I would love a garden with all my favorite fruits and vegetables, my life makes the commitment associated with the upkeep not practical for me. Maybe that will be part of my story when the pace of my life is slower and my kids have grown, living lives of their own. So, until then, I'm thankful for the farmers who can't see themselves doing anything else and truck drivers who enjoy driving to bring delicious produce to the grocery stores. I'm grateful for their service. I see it as a gift to society.

I saw an intriguing segment in the news about a man named Jamiah Hargins, founder of Crop Swap LA. His story intrigued me in four ways; his backstory, the catalyst for his organization, the emergence of his purpose, and the edification of his community through his gifts and his impetus to share it. I can't help to see how God would be pleased with his heart posture.

Jamiah's organization seeks to provide a solution to the disparity of living food in urban areas of Los Angeles. In his interview with Voyage LA, he shared that Crop Swap LA was born out of the need to provide his baby girl fresh, living food in the city of LA. He saw the injustice of this and began planting a garden in his backyard to provide for his family's needs. This is where his purpose and passion collided. However, the training ground and experience began during his time in Brazil, long before Crop Swap LA became a reality. In Brazil he helped manage a social enterprise that coordinated rural agriculture and local urban businesses to sustain a nearby orphanage's needs. His past experience served his current needs, and his passion gave birth to Crop Swap LA. According to his interview with Voyage LA, Crop Swap LA is "an organization that hires reentry citizens and veterans to build and maintain vegetable gardens on residential and commercial spaces."

What's more astonishing about Jamiah's story is that, at one time, he was a professional stock and options trader in Chicago. To see him now, I couldn't fathom that he once worked in the financial industry. When he talked about growing food, his whole countenance just lit up. You can tell this is a man who's living out his purpose. I got the impression Crop Swap LA is his mission, life purpose, and not toil or drudgery. I got the sense he wasn't dreaming of winning the lottery, so he could be delivered from his hellish job like so many who play the lottery, hoping to tender their resignation one day. What if we can identify our purpose through our story, our passions, and serve a need that will glorify God? What if we exchange a life doing a job that pays the bills but sucks the life out of us for a life on purpose that glorifies God, instead. How does living the days already numbered on this earth to live out more of what you were uniquely created for sound? Jamiah's gifts and purposes provide a significant service to his community.

Jamiah's story calls to mind two scriptures. The first is 1 Corinthians 12:12-30, which describes the diversity of gifts that we have that edifies the community. The Apostle Paul uses the analogy of our body. Our body has different parts, each part is significant, and the parts cannot operate independently from one another. I suspect he was prompted to remind the Corinthians that they weren't to be envious or quarrel about the various positions of service required for the church body's effectiveness. He reminds them they're all critical. All are necessary and different, and that's very good. In the second scripture, Acts 4: 32-35, we see an amazing picture of God's people gathering all their gifts and resources to edify and benefit their community.

Let's first look at *1 Corinthians* and see what we can learn and apply to our lives. Paul's letter to the church in Corinth offers this reminder:

> *For just as the body is one and has many members, and all the members of the body, though many, are one body, so it is with Christ. For in one Spirit, we were all baptized into one body—Jews or Greeks, slaves or free—and all were made to drink of one Spirit.*
> *For the body does not consist of one member but of many. If the foot should say, "Because I am not a hand, I do not belong to the body," that would not make it any less a part of the body. And if the ear should say, "Because I am not an eye, I do not belong to the body," that would not make it any less a part of the body. If the whole body were an eye, where would be the sense of hearing? If the whole body were an ear, where would be the sense of smell? But as it is, God arranged the members in the body, each one of them, as he chose. If all were a single member, where would the body be? As it is, there are many parts, yet one body.*

The eye cannot say to the hand, "I have no need of you," nor again the head to the feet, "I have no need of you." On the contrary, the parts of the body that seem to be weaker are indispensable, and on those parts of the body that we think less honorable we bestow the greater honor, and our unpresentable parts are treated with greater modesty, which our more presentable parts do not require. But God has so composed the body, giving greater honor to the part that lacked it, that there may be no division in the body, but that the members may have the same care for one another. If one member suffers, all suffer together; if one member is honored, all rejoice together. Now you are the body of Christ and individually members of it. And God has appointed in the church first apostles, second prophets, third teachers, then miracles, then gifts of healing, helping, administrating, and various kinds of tongues. Are all apostles? Are all prophets? Are all teachers? Do all work miracles? Do all possess gifts of healing? Do all speak with tongues? Do all interpret? (1 Corinthians 12:12-30)

Paul is referring to the inner workings and purpose of the church in Corinth. I want us to expand our view of this scripture to the kingdom of God at work in us, individually, as the church. Paul shared with the church the beauty and the necessity for everyone's genetic makeup, story, talents, abilities, and gifts to benefit the church. You, as the temple of God, the church, have been uniquely placed among your sphere of influence to bring your gift, no matter what it is, to build up the Kingdom of God. No need to compare yourself with others. No need to wish for something that you weren't created to do. No need to be something you're not. Not only are all the gifts that we bring important, but one isn't more important than the other. We all can't have the spotlight, nor should we want it if we weren't created for it. As a new mom, I was looking for a career that I could have that would allow me the flexibility to still mother my kids and generate a sizable income. At the time, the housing market was booming. My cousin was having great success as a realtor, so I got my realtor license. I worked hard and was dedicated, but I wasn't getting the results she was getting. I soon realized I wasn't passionate about selling homes. I was passionate about the idea of making money. After two years, I realized that while the intent was noble, I didn't enjoy looking at homes or showing homes, but I was around those who did. They were excited about seeing what was on the market, and all that comes with being a realtor. I, on the other hand, was not. It quickly became evident that real estate was neither my passion nor my calling. (What we do for a living to generate income may not necessarily be our purpose.)

Do you wish for a gift that's not your gifting? The sooner you embrace all that you have to offer, the more you'll operate in your giftings and thrive.

STEPS OF FAITH

- Look back at the things you did for convenience, approval, obligation, status, or whatever it may be for you and write it down.
- Pause for a moment. Accept that you desired something that wasn't designed for you. Take a moment to repent for coveting something that wasn't designed for you.
- Now, embrace what is for you. Ask God to forgive you for not being grateful for what He has given you as your gift. Thank Him for what He has given you. Rejoice! Take it in! Really, take it in! Hopefully, you're smiling at this new revelation.

Gifts to Benefit All

Chapter 4 of Acts displays a beautiful picture of the church bringing their resources and gifts to benefit all. What you bring to the table, which is you, benefits all. As we continue to see that, we, the church, have been created to benefit the Kingdom of God.

> *All the believers were one in heart and mind. No one claimed that any of their possessions was their own, but they shared everything they had. With great power the apostles continued to testify to the resurrection of the Lord Jesus. And God's grace was so powerfully at work in them*

all that there were no needy persons among them. For from time to time those who owned land or houses sold them, brought the money from the sales and put it at the apostles' feet, and it was distributed to anyone who had need.

(Acts 4:32-35 NIV)

We have tough times grasping our gifts and life isn't our own. We say things like it's my check, my money, my house, my life, etc. It's easy to adopt this mindset when our name is on the check, bank account statement, or deed. I worked for it and, therefore, it's mine to do with as I please. Well, we would be ill-informed because scriptures clearly state everything on earth and in heaven belongs to Him. Remember, He gave Adam and Eve dominion. They didn't give themselves dominion. In the United States, we have become a society where we lean more toward amassing so much and sharing little. The 2020 pandemic has been proof of that. Suddenly, toilet tissues became a hot commodity. No one saw that one coming! People were hoarding, a mindset of scarcity took root, and people couldn't see it in their hearts to share. Stores had to mandate a limit on toilet paper, disinfecting wipes, hand sanitizer, and water. Your gifts aren't only for you or to benefit you, which we can often forget. We take the very gifts, talents, and abilities and forget they were given to us to benefit all and glorify God. So, how can we take our gifts and resources to benefit and edify society and glorify God? That's the intention here. How can this be a win-win situation for all?

STEPS OF FAITH

- Write down how your offering/tribute, which is your purpose, can translate into something that will benefit not only you but also others and glorify God? Complete the following sentences.

  - My talents, abilities, gifts are
  _____

  - According to my story and passions, my purpose is
  _____

  - My purpose can benefit me, others by
  _____

  - God will be edified by
  _____

Now, with this added information and the realization that your gifts aren't for you alone but to bless God's creation and put Him on display, revisit what you thought your calling was and see if it needs fine-tuning or a complete overhaul. Rewrite your purpose calling. How do you feel? I hope a more authentic version of yourself emerges, and with that, a

PART V

clearer sense of direction. I celebrate with you on this journey of discovery.

You're made with purpose for a purpose!

PART VI

POSTURE:

Or do you not know that your body is a temple of the Holy Spirit within you, whom you have from God? You are not your own, for you were bought with a price. So glorify God in your body.

1 Corinthians 6:19-20 ESV

WE ARE MADE TO GLORIFY HIM

Bible scripture supports that we're created to glorify God with our lives. How does that statement make you feel? Let's try to understand the word "glory." The word is used many times in the Bible, but we can become detached from its meaning. What does it mean to glorify God with my life? For me it's acknowledging, respecting, and adoring God in the way I conduct myself. Since I'm made in His image, it pleases Him when I reflect His glory in what I say and do. I glorify Him in my praise and in worship of who He is.

As I mentioned, Moses' heart and passion for justice were already present. However, he went about it the wrong way. He sought to solve and bring about change to the things that grieved his heart through his strength and power when he killed the Egyptian slave driver. How is God glorified in that? God can't be glorified in that! Only Moses' can be glorified where he gets the accolades operating separately from God. Moses removed the slave driver his way; however, his way couldn't bring about the long-lasting change that God desired to give the Hebrew people. Moses' killing of the Egyptian slave driver couldn't offer the long-lasting deliverance that Moses hoped. He removed one slave driver, but another would soon take his place, therefore, rendering Moses' effort temporal. Only God could bring about the long-lasting change that's necessary.

We want our purpose, talents, abilities, giftings, and broken stories to glorify Him. Through the complete surrender of all the things that create our essence, God can take it and do above and beyond what we could ask or imagine. I don't know about you, but I want God to take my five loaves and two fish and feed thousands. I won't be able to do that by my human strength. I'll need the supernatural power of The One who created the universe and named the stars by name and knows the numbers of hairs on my head. Guess what? He wants that too! He wants to take your water and transform it into the best kind of wine. Far too often, we think we can do far better than God can do, so we rely on our efforts, and we fail to bring all that we're before the throne room of God to do what He will. Well, what does it look like to get all of what we're before the throne of God?

To move in faith is to not judge what is. It won't always make sense. It's hard for us to operate where our faith challenges us to look past the reality of the current situation. Yet, what makes a great inspirational movie is when all the odds are against the hero, and they somehow rise above it and thrive. I love the stories of the Olympic athletes. You hear of the story of Gabby

PART VI

Douglas, who was adopted and sacrificed and managed to overcome obstacles that would cause many to throw in the towel or remain hostage to their situations. Interestingly, kids have the innate gift to see beyond the realities of their surroundings. They can see the towel's potential to be a superhero cape when draped around their neck or to become their long sprawling hair when wrapped around their head. Their ability to believe, wonder, see, be in awe is something I'm going to invite us to revisit. We once had the ability to dream and wonder where there were no limits to the possibilities. Somehow, as we became older, we lost the awe and wonder we once possessed to dream, hope, and see past what is.

STEPS OF FAITH

- I want you to revisit the child in you who dreamt of being an astronaut, president, or anything you would blush to share now. Embrace this exercise. There might be something you may be able to glean from the child who was you. What did that exercise reveal to you?

It may seem silly, but it may reveal something about your essence that got trampled on before your guardian steered you to a calling. Maybe you were born in a long line of doctors, nurses, lawyers, politicians, teachers, a family business, or pastors and were expected to carry on the tradition. There's nothing wrong with any of these professions. If done well, they can give God much glory. When they're our God-given purpose, they become a calling rather than a job. I've raised four kids in a combination of school systems, so I can always spot the teachers who are merely there as a profession, a means to pay the bills rather than a calling. Sadly, only a handful of teachers I've encountered demonstrated a call to teaching. A disservice is done to kids' desire to learn when teachers aren't called, and it's apparent in their creativity to teach and their patience. I remember when I mentioned to my aunt that I wanted to study music, she suggested that I go into nursing as a backup plan. Well, my aunt's intention was well-meaning. She understood my pursuit would be challenging and unpredictable. A career in nursing offered more stability. After all, no one in my family of origin dared to pursue such a life. I was the oddball.

God gave us wisdom and the ability to reason for a purpose. We don't want to be foolish, but I think we could choke the power of God to do the miraculous and the supernatural when we don't leave any room for the power of the Holy Spirit to do what only the Holy Spirit can do.

PART VI

STEPS OF FAITH

- Where have you been led to what was necessary, practical, or expected instead of what you sensed was your God-given calling?
- What are your stories, strengths, passions, and abilities, but other voices clouded the truth of your God-given calling?
- Where has your inner brokenness talked you right out of your God-given calling?

Now that we processed our personal story and how it has shaped us through our spiritual story's lens, we should have identified what makes us unique. What are you drawn toward?

I want you to be thankful for every perceived setback, frustration, victory, and pain because all of it prompted new choices and new ways of operating to get you to choose something better. Congratulations! You're still standing. These experiences didn't break you, nor define you. They aren't the end of your story. What's interesting about being in the valley is that while you're in the valley, it seems so unbearable you can't wait to overcome the pain. Still, when you overcome, you can't help celebrate and give God glory for what He allowed you to overcome. You reflect with gratitude for the lessons learned; at least, you should. Make it a practice to see these challenging and sometimes painful parts of your story with appreciation. Hopefully, you can see that God will never leave you or forsake you, and with belief, determination, and perseverance, you can overcome. What comes immediately to mind is after the Israelites crossed the Red Sea, they witnessed the destruction of the Egyptians who were intent on killing them. When victory was clear to them, they were jubilant that their God had rescued them. They began singing, dancing, and playing instruments. Before their survival, victory was uncertain; however, they believed with determination and persevered anyway. They persevered and escaped from the mighty Egyptians with all their chariots, manpower, and weapons.

How were these slaves able to accomplish such a feat? Everything seemed to work against them. Indeed, they were no match for the mighty Egyptians, but what they did have was the I AM God who loved them, who would fight for them and intercede on their behalf. I want you to know that the God of old is the same God who loves you with that same love. He intends to love you, correct you, fight for you, and intercede on your behalf. His plan for you is for your good. He doesn't relish when His children are suffering and not thriving. It grieves His heart.

So, no regrets, and it's never too late. No talk of "should haves" or "if onlys." Remove that way of thinking and replace it with "I'm wiser, sharper, and better equipped for this part of my life" because all these statements are more trustworthy. I love that even though Moses took matters into his own hands by killing the Egyptian, took a detour, and delayed his calling until he was eighty years old, he still fulfilled it. It may have seemed too late to some, given his age. However, God's timing is perfect. I like to think those forty years were packed with lessons that prepared him for the calling at eighty. He probably was less impetuous at eighty than he was at forty. I'm sure God can better use a Moses at eighty than a Moses at forty who is strong-willed. I know that I'm better equipped today for life's challenges than I would have been at twenty years old. God's timing is perfect! Say it to yourself! "God's timing is perfect, and I'm right where I should be. Arriving at this point in my life too early would just leave me ill-prepared."

I want you to take all that you've learned, reflected, and brought before the Lord to inform what your purpose is. Through this process, I've identified what my purpose is: to encourage women to see themselves as God sees them and help them realize that great truth in a tangible way. I distilled this discovery to one bold statement: Encourage and empower women to be all that God created them to be! As I reflected, on my history and where I chose to invest my time in service it was always with women. I found great joy in seeing women experience breakthroughs and restorations. Now, I want you to write your bold statement.

STEPS OF FAITH

- Again, does your purpose statement need any editing? Or does it evoke a sense of excitement, assurance and calm?
- Write down your purpose statement? Don't judge it!

I want you to sit with what you've written and rejoice because you've taken an enormous step of clarity and knowing. It may seem overwhelming and scary to say what your calling is out loud verbally, but I want you to do just that. Say it OUT LOUD! How did that feel? Embrace it! Now ask God what He wants you to do in light of this new realization. Maybe this journey confirmed what you already knew. I celebrate with you. If you still aren't clear what your purpose is. Don't fret. Spend some time understanding all your story: the good, bad, and ugly of it through the lens of our mighty God. Ask Him how He may want to use your story's unique aspects to bring about redemption and give Him glory. Spend some time listening quietly and asking.

I want to offer this bit of advice if you're still confused or unsure of your calling. Don't get frustrated. You're right where you need to be, and it may take a little time. Enjoy the journey! Often, we want the diploma without any of the work. We want it now! We want to find shortcuts. I've learned that shortcuts only do yourself a disservice; shortcuts cut you short of the fullness of your purpose. I want to take the pressure off naming your calling. When we use the term" purpose" or "calling," we can add so much more pressure than is necessary. Our purpose can be something we're already doing. Our calling can be as simple as obedience and consistency to the daily and maybe mundane tasks that won't provide recognition or accolades from the masses, but delight God's heart. It may be the obedience in what seems a small thing of taking care of your aging parents. It may be rearing your kids to their purpose. Remember Hannah and Puah, the Hebrew midwives? Their purpose was associated with what they were already doing. They had a significant impact on the survival of the male Israelites boys. Rahab provided an escape for the spies, which may look insignificant, but had a huge impact on Israel's victory in Jericho, which allowed her to be grafted into Jesus' genealogy. Mary's acceptance to carry the long-awaited Messiah in her womb may seem small, but her cooperation with the Holy Spirit had long-lasting implications that we still benefit from until Jesus returns. The parents who birthed Martin Luther King Jr. aren't mentioned, but I'm sure they were instrumental in forming a young Martin. The calling to parents may seem insignificant and can be overlooked but necessary. We might have missed the impact of so many well-known figures who have left an impact on our society long after they left this earth if it hadn't been for those parents who were cultivating their brilliance. Again, don't judge or compare your calling to anyone else. Listen carefully to what God is whispering to you. I tell you, in that realization, you'll experience joy, significance, and purpose that we all are searching for and only a few experiences. Let's be counted as the ones living on purpose, edifying others, and glorifying God.

Allow God to whisper to you how he wants to use your life to benefit others and glorify HIm.

STEPS OF FAITH

- My purpose is to _____ to edify _____ for the glory of God.

- My purpose is to _____ to share my redemption story of _____ to the glory of God.

You Are Made With Purpose for a Purpose!

PART VII

BATTLE READY:

Submit yourselves therefore to God.
Resist the devil, and he will flee from you.

James 4:7 ESV

PUT ON YOUR ARMOR

There's an enemy that Does Not want you to fulfill the plans that God has already preordained for you.

Prepare for Battle

When September 11th hit the shores of the United States in 2001, it was a wake-up call. We realized that we weren't immune to terrorism. We also gained some insight into how these particular terrorists operate and think. We became more familiar with how they do warfare. Therefore, we became more aware of how we need to protect ourselves, fight, and defeat this enemy to the United States.

We need to know a few things about our enemy. If you don't think you have an enemy, I'm afraid you've left yourself open to being a soft target. How does this enemy operate? And what weapons or defense mechanisms are necessary and available to us? So, who is our enemy? Do we have an enemy? Is it all in my head? Well, the Bible clearly states that there's an enemy whose sole purpose is to kill, steal, and destroy. That's what he tried to do to Adam and Eve and attempted to do to

Jesus. If this enemy, who is against the plans of God and the plans for your life, had the audacity to tempt Jesus, the King of kings, and the Lords of lords, then he won't hesitate to go after you.

How will he try to destroy you? It's interesting that Satan, "The father of lies," knows something about us; otherwise, he wouldn't be so good at tempting us to go against God. The enemy knows that we have a tendency and desire to want to be God of our lives. We see the evidence of this with Adam and Eve. The conversation between Eve and the Serpent, "the father of lies," gives us some insight into our hearts, the way the enemy works, and the TRUTH. Let's look at Genesis where we see the first mention of Satan and his crafty ways.

> *Now the serpent was more cunning than any beast of the field which the Lord God had made. And he said to the woman, "Has God indeed said, 'You shall not eat of every tree of the garden'?"*
> *And the woman said to the serpent, "We may eat the fruit of the trees of the garden; but of the fruit of the tree which is in the midst of the garden, God has said, 'You shall not eat it, nor shall you touch it, lest you die.'"*
> *Then the serpent said to the woman, "You will not surely die. For God knows that in the day you eat of it your eyes will be opened, and you will be like God, knowing good and evil."*
> *So when the woman saw that the tree was good for food, that it was pleasant to the eyes, and a tree desirable to*

make one wise, she took of its fruit and ate. She also gave to her husband with her, and he ate. Then the eyes of both of them were opened, and they knew that they were naked: and they sewed fig leaves together and made themselves coverings.
And they heard the sound of the Lord God walking in the garden in the cool of the day, and Adam and his wife hid themselves from the presence of the Lord God among the trees of the garden."

(Genesis 3:1-8 NKJV)

The chapter opens with a clue to the serpent's character. He is cunning. In some Bible translations, they describe him as crafty. The words "cunning" and "crafty" paint a picture of someone who will do and say anything to bring about their ultimate plan. He'll use whatever means necessary. He doesn't have a conscience for what's right. He'll spout lies as truth and will convince you of the same. And the troubling part is the enemy will gain success with this strategy. His lies will be so convincing that you'll doubt yourself, what you heard, what you know about yourself, and, most importantly, the truth about what God says about you. That's why we took so much time revisiting some of our trauma and pain, sifted through them, and put them in their proper perspective. When the thing that has the power to destroy is brought out in the open, it loses its purpose. Why? Because the enemy knows you. He'll attempt to utilize your weakness against you; thus, you need to know your weak points, so when your enemy tries to use these tender points of your story as a weapon against you, you can stop it in its tracks. Let's use Superman, a fictional character, as an example. He knew he was strong, but he also needed to know that he had in him a place of weakness. If he doesn't acknowledge this, he leaves himself exposed to be destroyed. He leaves his enemies with an upper hand.

When superheroes first recognize they have a superpower, they begin exploring every aspect of their superpower and capabilities. They embark on a journey to understand what they possess. They learn new levels of their superpower. They begin to harness this power by fine-tuning and strengthening their powers so they can use it at its optimum capacity. But guess what? As they explore every aspect of their power, they also learn the limitations of their power and their weakness. My sisters, whom I love so much, and I know, without a doubt, love me too, knew me so well, and I knew them too. As kids, when we found ourselves arguing about something silly, we knew each other's pressure points if we wanted to take out our opponent in battle. There was a point where we would go for the jugular and hit a weak point that we knew was a sore spot for the other, and the mere mention may render our opponent paralyzed to take them out. Our loved ones know these spots so well because they know our weaknesses. I see it with my kids. They love each other, but now and again, one goes too far and hits the other's sore spot on purpose. This is how marriages become casualties. The Bible says the mysterious gift of marriage is that two people become one person. That's why the information we have amassed during our time in marriage has the potential to torpedo a marriage if not careful. Well, when our loving Father brings about our sore spots to the forefront, His desire is to bring healing and restoration, unlike the enemy, who seeks to use it against you. So far, the work you've done to identify these sore spots has put you a few steps ahead of the enemy.

Next, we learn that God created the enemy. What? Why would God create such a thing! We know that everything God created from every living thing and the creation of human beings was very good. So how is Satan possible? Well, Satan is possible because God gives us a choice. He desires us to trust Him and believe Him, and He longs for us to invite Him into our lives. He will never impose His will on our lives. We all have the same access to Him. In Isaiah 14: 12 and Ezekiel 28: 12-14, we find that Satan, otherwise known as the "Adversary," was once an angel who dwelled in heaven with God until he desired not only to be like God, but to be God. I say this often to my kids, "play your position," meaning we all can't be the captain. There can only be one main chef or coach, hence, only one mama. If I have to make a decision, I may entertain some input, but, at the end of the day, when I make the executive decision, discussion is closed. Satan couldn't and wouldn't accept that his position as an angel was to further the agenda of the Almighty God. Here are two passages of scripture that tell us something about Satan.

> *How you are fallen from heaven,*
> *O shining star, son of the morning!*
> *You have been thrown down to the earth,*
> *you who destroyed the nations of the world.*
> *For you said to yourself,*
> *'I will ascend to heaven and set my throne above God's stars.*
> *I will preside on the mountain of the gods*
> *far away in the north.*
> *I will climb to the highest heavens*
> *and be like the Most High.*

(Isaiah 14:12-14)

And,

> *You were the anointed cherub who covers;*
> *I established you;*
> *You were on the holy mountain of God;*
> *You walked back and forth in the midst of fiery stones.*

PART VII

You were perfect in your ways from the day you were created,
Till iniquity was found in you.
"By the abundance of your trading
You became filled with violence within,
And you sinned;
Therefore I cast you as a profane thing
Out of the mountain of God;
And I destroyed you, O covering cherub,
From the midst of the fiery stones.

(Ezekiel 28: 14-16)

So, we see how Satan came to be. He wanted to be God and the god of his life. In Chapter 3, verse 1 of Genesis, he tells the woman, *"Has God indeed said, 'You shall not eat of every tree of the garden'?" (NKJV).* We see Satan's craftiness at work. He infuses doubt and confusion. Let's not overlook that he knows what God said. Remember that Satan knows scripture. He knows how God operates; after all, he was in the presence of the Lord of lords. So, Satan comes into the picture, knowing a bit about God and us. Satan can take what he knows and cultivate an avenue of temptation, disobedience, and distrust for God.

In verse 2, we see Eve respond to the serpent with what she knew to be true. And it was the truth! She says, *"We may eat the fruit of the trees of the garden; but of the fruit of the tree which is in the midst of the garden, God has said, 'You shall not eat it, nor shall you touch it, lest you die'" (NKJV)*. Aha! Eve wasn't confused, so how did the serpent convince her to mistrust God who provided everything she needed for her and Adam. How could she mistrust the God she dwelt with who proved faithful repeatedly, who had their best interest at heart? Well, let's look at the serpent's response to Eve, *"You will not surely die. For God knows that in the day you eat of it, your eyes will be opened, and you will be like God, knowing good and evil" (NKJV)*. Satan begins with a lie. He calls God a liar when he said, "You will not surely die," something God said would happen to them. And then Satan follows it up with temptation and more lies in verse five. The serpent makes Eve believe that God is withholding something from her by convincing her that God doesn't want her to be like Him when we know God already made us in His likeness. And while we're made in His image and likeness, we can never be God, nor do we want to be. It's too great a weight we weren't designed for, and that's when we encounter issues when we try to be God of our lives. We need to know how to play our position. We believe our lives are our own to do what we wish with statements like, "It's my life!" and our favorite "Don't tell me what to do!" We Americans love this one the most. We have the right to, and you can fill the blank. Don't get me wrong; we do have rights because

PART VII

God gave us an amazing gift to partner with Him in dominion and authority over all that He has created. However, He didn't give us dominion and authority over one another; that, my friend, is a right reserved for God alone. Maybe if we can remember to let God be Judge overall and play our position well, which is to love God with all our heart and love our neighbors as ourselves, I suspect we could solve many of the issues that ail us and plague our society.

So finally, we see the serpent succeed in convincing Eve to eat the fruit. In verses 5 and 6, we see her thought process and the outcome of her decision.

So when the woman saw that the tree was good for food, that it was pleasant to the eyes, and a tree desirable to make one wise, she took of its fruit and ate. She also gave to her husband with her, and he ate. Then the eyes of both of them were opened, and they knew that they were naked; and they sewed fig leaves together and made themselves coverings."

(Genesis 3: 5-6 NKJV)

She now is tempted by the look of the fruit. She may have walked by that fruit tree many times and had no interest until the serpent presented it to her as something that she's missing and has every right to partake. I find it interesting when I'm eating something; my kids have no interest until they see me eating it. Suddenly, they want some too. It was the same way with their toys. They'll have no interest in a toy until one of the siblings shows an interest; then, suddenly, everyone wants to play with it at that moment. But what really is quite telling about what made her disobey God and ultimately made her believe that God didn't have their best interest when all He has done proved that He, indeed, had their best intentions. She saw *"that the tree was desirable to make one wise" (Genesis 3: 5 NKJV)*. Aha! There it is! She, too, wanted to be God. She ate the serpent's poisonous lies and desire to be God.

STEPS OF FAITH

- Where have you become God of your life?
- Where have you usurped the position of God, believing that His plans and instructions aren't for your good?
- Where do you believe He is withholding something from you? Where do you treat God more like your servant to do your bidding rather than the Most High God?

We finally see the consequence of Adam and Eve's disobedience. The serpent did tell the truth about one thing. Their eyes were opened, and they were able to know the difference between good and evil, but they were indeed experiencing death that the enemy assured them they wouldn't experience. They didn't physically die. However, death came in the form of shame, fear, broken trust, blame, and, most importantly, a severed relationship with God that wouldn't allow them to walk with God in the cool of the day as they were accustomed.

So, why was it necessary to learn Satan's backstory? It's important, so we know how the adversary of our God operates. Satan isn't interested in you but rather how he can destroy the master plan of the Most High God. Satan doesn't want God to receive the glory that will come from your obedience to the purpose He has deposited in your heart.

Hold captive the Internal Thoughts and External Speech

Your adversary:

- wants you to doubt what you know God has told you
- wants to take the pain of your story and use it against you
- wants to exploit your desires so that you desire them more than God
- wants you to receive the lies whispered to you as a child as truth

- wants you to think *Who am I to* _____ ?
  (You fill in the blank.)
- wants you to throw in the towel
- wants you to use excuses like I'm too old
- wants you to use excuses like I'm too young
- wants you to use excuses like I'm too busy
- wants you to use excuses like I don't know enough
- wants you to use excuses like I don't have the resources to _____
- wants you to be your worst enemy by self-sabotaging God's plan for you
- wants you to procrastinate
- wants you to remain in fear
- wants you to play it safe

Let's not give our adversary, "the father of lies," the serpent, our enemy, Satan, the victory.

Here's what I want you to know. Repeat it if you have to:

- I am already victorious.
- My Father in heaven fights for me; all I need to do is stand firm as He fights.
- My God will equip me for every situation.
- I am God's masterpiece. He made me with thought and purpose.
- God's love for me is so wide, high, and deep.

- Nothing I can say or do can separate me from the love of God as His beloved.
- My God will NEVER leave me or forsake me... that's His promise.
- God's promises are worthy of my trust.
- I won't rely on what I see because I have a God working behind the scenes on my behalf.
- My God has a plan for me that's for my good.
- Satan is a defeated foe. Satan is no match for our Mighty God.
- If God is for me, therefore, no one or nothing can come against me!

The statements above have scripture woven into each statement. When Satan was tempting Jesus in the Garden of Gethsemane, He used scripture to combat every lie the devil tried to hurl at Him. In Luke 4: 1-12, Jesus responded to each temptation and lie with, "It is written." Jesus is giving us a clue as to how we, too, can defeat the temptation and lies of the adversary. Jesus, we know, is fully man and fully God. He could have avoided temptation, but He allowed Himself as a man to endure the temptation to restore what was broken in the Garden of Eden with Adam and Eve. So, we too can defeat the enemy with the power of scripture.

STEPS OF FAITH

- Write down every lie you replay in your mind and replace it with the truth of God, the scriptures.

If fear, anxiety, unbelief, lack-mindset, low self-esteem, etc. are your nemesis, then combat each lie with scripture. I assure you there's a scripture for each lie we convince ourselves is real. Commit these scriptures to memory, so when each lie surfaces when you're being triggered, immediately recite scripture over yourself like a healing balm. I assure you, with time, these lies will lose their power. And when the enemy tries to reignite these lies, you'll know what to do. Oh yes, the enemy is relentless. He'll return when you've overcome his lies with truth. *Luke 4: 13 NKJV* says, *"Now when the devil had ended every temptation, he departed from Him until an opportune time."* This scripture clearly states that Satan would attempt to tempt Jesus again. You would think the devil would get a clue, but he's too full of himself that he's relentless in his pursuit to be God. Let me let you in on another secret if you don't already know. Satan is defeated by Jesus forever, so while we wait for this prophetic truth to be fulfilled, you're at an advantage. We know how the story ends. We'll be victorious! We are victorious! So, my beloved, don't allow the enemy, our adversary, to convince you otherwise.

PART VII

In the book of Job, Satan mentions to God that Job is only faithful, because...., so that means that Satan has some insight about Job. Satan knew what God told Adam and Eve. How does he know these things? My best guess is because he was once an angel, and angels are given the freedom to move about the heavenly realm and the earthly realm. Satan is foolish and arrogant enough even to try to tempt Jesus, so he won't think twice to tempt you. That says a lot about Satan. He is full of himself. Could you imagine the audacity of Satan to tempt God the Son? While Satan knows a few things. He has limited power. He can't touch one hair on your person without permission from our loving Father. That's evident in the book of Job.

Let's end this chapter by talking about some other gear that makes for a perfect armor.

Finally, my brethren, be strong in the Lord and in the power of His might. Put on the whole armor of God, that you may be able to stand against the wiles of the devil. For we do not wrestle against flesh and blood, but against principalities, against powers, against the rulers of the darkness of this age, against spiritual hosts of wickedness in the heavenly places. Therefore take up the whole armor of God, that you may be able to withstand in the evil day, and having done all, to stand.
Stand therefore, having girded your waist with truth, having put on the breastplate of righteousness, and having

shod your feet with the preparation of the gospel of peace; above all, taking the shield of faith with which you will be able to quench all the fiery darts of the wicked one. And take the helmet of salvation, and the sword of the Spirit, which is the word of God; praying always with all prayer and supplication in the Spirit, being watchful to this end with all perseverance and supplication for all the saints—and for me, that utterance may be given to me, that I may open my mouth boldly to make known the mystery of the gospel, for which I am an ambassador in chains; that in it I may speak boldly, as I ought to speak.

(Ephesians 6:10-20)

Paul, the author of Ephesians, implores us to put on not just any armor but the armor of God and to acknowledge that we have an adversary who is like a lion that seeks to devour us because he plans to kill, steal, and destroy God's plans for our life. We are going to ensure we have every piece of God's armor so we can stand firm in temptation and "speak boldly, as I ought to speak." Well, what does the armor of God include? We see the armor of God consists of six significant pieces of clothing necessary for battle. You don't want to go to battle without any of these pieces. Some components of the armor will be used more than others, depending on the need, but all must be worn, so we're ready to use what we need when we need it and ensure effectiveness.

Belt of truth

In biblical times, soldiers wore a tunic, and over the tunic, they wore a belt that would adjust the length of the tunic to prevent them from falling. It also housed the weapons they would carry to battle. So, what can we take away from verse 14, which says to "gird your waist with truth"? According to the Oxford Languages, gird means "to prepare oneself for something difficult or challenging," which leads me to think we should be prepared for an attack that will require truth as our weapon, but not just any "truth," but the truth of God. This further confirms that when the enemy comes to confuse you or plant doubts and lies into your thoughts about who you are, combat every poisonous lie with the truth of who God says you are. This truth remains the same yesterday, today, and tomorrow. It's immovable! It will never change like the fashion and culture of the day.

Breastplate of Righteousness

The breastplate covers the essential organs of your body. In biblical times the breastplate covered the base of the neck to the thighs. It protects your heart, lungs, stomach, kidney, and liver from any sharp weapons. The most important organ, in my opinion, is the heart. The breastplate protects and deflects. The heart is mentioned numerous times in the Bible. We're told to guard our hearts; it's mentioned in several scriptures that God knows our hearts. We can never fool God because He knows our hearts. I sense we're told to protect our hearts with the righteousness that doesn't come from anything we do but rather the righteousness that we inherit from accepting the work of Jesus on the cross. We're righteous because of what Jesus did on the cross, and not by any amount of money we donated, volunteer hours we've accumulated, or even the impact of our ministries. So, Jesus' righteousness deflects any arrows the enemy may want to unleash. Let the breastplate of righteousness deflect shame, guilt, low self-esteem, fear, or other unhealthy emotions that may render us paralyzed. The righteousness of Jesus will inform our behavior. None of our poor choices, sin if you will, or what was spoken over you is the pillar of your story. You have inherited the righteousness of God, which protects your heart from yourself and those who might bring up your past. Remember, you have the Breastplate of Righteousness. That should bring a smile to your face and confidence.

Shoes of the Gospel of Peace

Back then, walking was the main form of transportation. It would have been necessary to have shoes to protect your feet from the rough terrain of the day. People walked everywhere, unlike today. In Greek, the word "*eirene*" mentioned in this passage means peacemaker, quietness, rest, set at one again. A further meaning is to reconcile, to be at peace, and to make peace. I love that it means to reconcile because we have spent quite a bit of time reconciling our past that we have inherited and lived with to embrace the peace that comes from accepting and appreciating every part of our story.

I'm sure you've heard this saying: "hurt people hurt people." When you're hurt, there's no way you can be at peace and bring peace to whatever you do and wherever you go. We want to embody peace, bring peace, and make peace. Peace brings about a healthy, strong, and sound mind. So, wherever you go, contend to bring the authenticity of who you are. All of who you are, which is the earthly part of your story, filled with brokenness and joy, and your story's spiritual aspect. This reveals the most authentic part of your story intended to lead you to wholeness and peace. Jesus tells his disciples He is going to leave, but he will leave them an Advocate, Holy Spirit, that will not only comfort them but bring them a peace that He brought wherever He went. *"Peace I leave with you; my peace I give you. I do not give to you as the world gives. Do not let your hearts be troubled and do not be afraid" (John 14:27 NIV).* So, allow God to lead you wherever He places you or leads you with the peace He brings. You'll need that peace as you bring about the purpose planted within you into fruition.

Shield of Faith

The shield is a defensive weapon designed to protect and shield yourself from attackers and flying projectiles such as arrows from the enemy. Paul says, *"Above all, taking the shield of faith with which you will be able to quench all the fiery darts of the wicked one" (Ephesians 6:16 KJV)*. I'm intrigued by what he says, "above all." This leads me to think that this particular gear is especially necessary. We know that faith is a key component in believing in God. To believe and have faith in God you cannot see requires a belief that goes above what the intellectual mind can comprehend. However, we operate in faith, whether we realize it or not. When we cast our ballot to vote for the presidency, we're putting our trust and confidence in that person. We put our faith in what that person said they would do. We are operating in faith that what they have promised will be kept.

So, what's Paul encouraging us to in this passage? Two things are clear to me: we're to put our trust and confidence in God's truthfulness, "The Word," and rely wholeheartedly on the salvation we have in Christ. So, grab your shield of faith knowing without equivocation that your faith in the God who created you has equipped you with the Bible, a love story of the pursuit of you, filled with truth about who you are and who your Creator is to fend off every fiery dart Satan and his agents will try to hurl at you. We have already established that the devil, your adversary assignment is to destroy every perfect plan God has for you, to kill and steal your dreams and purposes of God. I love that Paul assures that "the shield of faith will be able to "quench all the fiery darts of the wicked one." The shield of faith will extinguish and put out not some of the fiery darts but ALL of the fiery darts. Take that in! This further confirms the power of the word and the exercise I offered to you to help undo every lie you have spoken over yourself or was spoken over you intentionally or subliminally. I say subliminally because one of the sins of the United States is slavery. I had to come to terms with how I accepted the subliminal message that would lead me to believe that I'm inferior, less than. I need to adapt to the social construct established as right and leave me subliminally accepting these lies straight from the pit of hell as truth. I accepted it as part of the society that I live in, and to succeed in it, I needed to adapt and play along to get along. I realize now it was a survival mechanism that I adopted. But was I really surviving? I soon realized pieces of me were being shattered. How can one thrive authentically in wholeness in a system in opposition to the perfect plan of our Holy and All-Knowing God? Christians will have to come to terms with their participation in upholding this in God's holy temple, the church. So, my friend, we know that *"For our struggle is not against flesh and blood, but against the rulers, against the authorities, against the powers of this dark world and against the spiritual forces of evil in the heavenly realms" (Ephesians 6:12).* The accuser, our adversary will stop at nothing to use everything, anything, and anyone to destroy God's perfect, masterful plan, and you're part of that plan. So be courageous and grab your shield of faith.

Helmet of Salvation and Sword of the Spirit

I'm pairing the helmet and the sword together because Paul connects them in verse 17, *"And take the helmet of salvation, and the sword of the Spirit, which is the word of God."* It seems to me pairing them together makes them more effective and most potent. And we want to be the most effective and powerful when we go into battle.

Today, we wear a helmet whether we're bike riding, motorcycle, or skateboarding to prevent head trauma in a collision. Roman soldiers of Paul's day would have worn a helmet to protect their heads from sharp objects like a spear or sword.

So, we're told to "take the helmet," some Bible versions say, "Put on the helmet," while most lean toward "Take." According to Strong's Concordance, the word "take" in Greek is *dechomai* (pronounced dekh'-om-ahee) means to receive, accept, take. There seems to be a responsibility on our part to not simply put the helmet on, but to receive and accept the helmet of salvation and all that it offers. According to the Oxford

PART VII

Languages, salvation means preservation or deliverance from harm, ruin, or loss. The Salvation we receive from Jesus rescued us from ourselves and the enemy that intends to destroy us. He preserved us from harm, ruin, and loss—the harm and loss of being separated from a good God. The salvation Jesus purchased for us is a reconciliation to God the Father, the Creator. I don't think we fully comprehend the ramifications of our disconnection from The Source of our being. It would be like a child not connected to the placenta that connects the mother to the baby, designed to provide the baby all that it needs to thrive in its mother's womb to be healthy and whole. If we go back to when God told Adam and Eve that if they eat the fruit, they'll surely die, once they did eat the fruit, their relationship that they once enjoyed with God in its fullness was severed, but thankfully, not forever. They were cast out of the safety that they enjoyed being in the presence that God provided. The only way to restore what was severed would be the sacrifice Jesus offered by willingly being the sin offering forevermore. All we need to do is accept this salvation that will protect our mind, our thoughts from the attack of the enemy, the accuser.

The sword can be a defensive and offensive weapon, but the only offensive weapon mentioned in the armor. The sword can deflect a weapon, or it can initiate an attack on your enemy. The Roman soldier would hold the sword in their right hand while holding the shield in his left. The sword would rest in his belt until he needed it for battle. It was a nice size length, not too small, not too big to hinder, but the right size and light enough to pull out at a moment's notice to puncture their adversary. So, what does Paul mean by *"take... the sword of the Spirit, which is the word of God."* As we revisit the word "take," you want to receive and accept the Spirit, which is the Word of God. The Spirit, The Word, and God are synonymous. We know this is one of God's mysteries, which is that God is three distinct persons in one: God the Father, God the Son, and God the Holy Spirit. All distinctly different, yet One is working perfectly in unison, not contradicting or opposing the other.

The Holy Spirit, we know, gives human beings courage, strength, and boldness, among other things. We know when David was chosen and anointed by Samuel, the Holy Spirit came upon him, *"And the Spirit of the Lord rushed upon David from that day forward. And Samuel rose and went to Ramah" (1 Samuel 16:13).* David exudes all three, courage, strength, and boldness, to defeat Goliath. He was the least likely to defeat Goliath. He was a little boy with no military background. He possessed nothing at first glance that would convince anyone that he would be victorious in defeating Goliath, yet he did. Goliath was so certain he was going to destroy this nice-looking boy. However, this is the response of David,

You are coming against me with sword, spear, and javelin, but I come against you in the name of the Lord Almighty, the God of the Israelite armies, which you have defied. This very day the Lord will put you in my power; I will defeat you and cut off your head. And I will give the bodies of the Philistine soldiers to the birds and animals to eat. Then the whole world will know that Israel has a God, and everyone here will see that the Lord does not need swords or spears to save his people. He is victorious in battle, and he will put all of you in our power.

(1 Samuel 17: 45-47 NIV)

Wow! Bold statements to make from a young David. However, David understood his courage and boldness, and ultimate victory in battle resulted from the power of the Holy Spirit working within him and for him.

The Book of Judges gives an account that Samson is chosen by God and given a physical strength that baffles all that see him. The Philistines were baffled and puzzled as to why Samson possessed the strength and power he demonstrated. I imagine it was in part to the strength he possessed that was incongruent to his actual physicality. It probably didn't make sense. He probably looked like every other guy. He probably wasn't a giant or muscular in stature, and yet he possessed this strength. Another reminder that God sees differently than we see, uses whom he chooses, and does miraculous things that baffle humankind.

> *But the Lord said, to Samuel when selecting a young David as future king, "Do not look on his appearance or the height of his stature, because I have rejected him. For the Lord sees not as man sees; man looks on the outward appearance, but the Lord looks on the heart."*
>
> (1 Samuel 16: 7-8)

Samson, who once was filled with the power of the Holy Spirit, experienced the departure of the Holy Spirit; poor choices and disobedience caused him to be tragically captured by the Philistines and suffer the shame of having his eyes gouged at the hands of the Philistines. However, we see both God's mercy and his humility when his final request before he took his final breath to God was to have the Spirit of God fill him one last time to destroy his enemy and enemy of God. With the power of the Holy Spirit dwelling inside him, he destroys his enemies instantly.

In Acts, we see Peter filled with the Holy Spirit's power, which enables him to be bold, courageous, and full of power preaching the gospel despite the threat of imprisonment and death. This was the same Peter who denied Jesus for fear of his life after Jesus' capture. This is a small indication of the magnitude of power that the Holy Spirit is capable of and that we who have accepted Jesus have dwelling inside of us. We want to use and operate fully in the power of the Holy Spirit. As I mentioned before, scriptures say the same Spirit that resurrected Jesus is the same one that lives within us. You see how the Helmet of Salvation and the Sword of Spirit pair make the armor impenetrable. The Salvation given to us by Jesus and the power of the Holy Spirit makes us hard to be defeated. This doesn't mean we won't be in battle, but when you find yourself in battle, put on the armor of God and remind yourself of the arsenal that's at your disposal. Our God fights for and goes before us. You'll be able to withstand the enemy's attacks because God has already set you up for victory. Now believe it!

Paul, imprisoned for the faith, encourages his fellow believers to put on the armor of God by praying in the Spirit. Praying in the Spirit enables him to speak boldly,

> *always praying with all prayer and supplication in the Spirit, being watchful to this end with all perseverance and supplication for all the saints— and for me, that utterance may be given to me, that I may open my mouth boldly to make known the mystery of the gospel, for which I'm an ambassador in chains; that in it I may speak boldly, as I ought to speak.*
>
> (Ephesians 6:18-20)

I have prayed for you already, and I encourage you to pray as God's purpose for your life becomes clear to you, so you're empowered to move boldly as you ought to.

You were made with purpose for a purpose!

PART VIII

LACKING NOTHING:

For the Lord God is a sun and shield; The Lord will give grace and glory;
No good thing will He withhold from those who walk uprightly.

Psalms 119: 105 ESV

EQUIPPED WITH ALL THAT YOU NEED

I like the lyrics of the song "It's Not Over" by Israel Houghton and New Breed.

If God is in it

There is no limit...

I love music. Music has the power to change your perspective, encourage, lift your spirits, and bring joy. In Broadway musicals, the characters are often moved to break out into song because mere words aren't enough to express everything that's felt. I feel the same way about God's Word and truth set to music! Scriptures and worship songs possess the power to remind me of what's true and right about me when my insecurities and baggage threaten to hold me back from all that God wants to do through me. When my baggage, insecurities, and the lies of this world want to convince me that it's over. It's a wrap! Your best days are behind you! You're too old! You missed your opportunity to have an impact on the way God wanted to use you. Does any of it sound remotely familiar? If it does, I want to tell you it's a lie straight from the pit of hell.

I want to tell you, "It's not over until God says so..." a lyric from the song "It Ain't Over" by Maurette Brown Clark. We tend to focus on our human limitations rather than shift our focus to The One who is All-Powerful, All-Knowing, Omnipresent and Omniscient, God. We need to remember, "If God is in it, there is no limit." My friend, we want God to be in everything and anything that we touch or a part of because then we can be sure of the unlimited possibility in God. We want a long-lasting impact that still has an impact long after we've taken our last breath. We don't want an impact that's here today and gone tomorrow. I want you to know that God also wants to use you and equip you for His maximum impact. I don't want to work hard. I want to work smart, and working smart means inviting God on the journey.

I'm drawn to Caleb and Joshua's story in Numbers. Moses sends one person from each of the twelve tribes to spy out Canaan at God's command. In this account, we see how there are two emerging perspectives that the twelves spies witnessed and what they ended up reporting as a reality. The perspective you bring to your purpose and every situation you'll find yourself in will be critical. Your perspective will impact how you move about your life and the world in which you live. It will ultimately affect the impact God wants to have on your mission.

So, the twelve go and spies out Canaan, and after forty days of their exploration, they return to give a report that will seal their fate. They confirm that the land indeed flows with milk and honey as promised by God. They even brought fruit from the bounty of the land, but soon after, we see how the perspectives quickly change and affect their report to Moses, Aaron, and the community. *"But the people who live there are powerful, and the cities are fortified and very large. We even saw descendants of Anak there" (Numbers 13:28 NIV).* They believe they can't defeat the Canaanites; they gave more credence to the might and power to the people they saw than the God who has tabernacled with them showed Himself worthy of their trust and belief. Their assessment of their ability to defeat the inhabitants of Canaan and descendants of Anak, who were giants, quickly spread fear and doubt throughout the whole community. However, Caleb silenced the congregation and told Moses, "We should go up and take possession of the land, for we can certainly do it" (Numbers 13:30 NIV) Then Joshua and Caleb attempted to convince the people who wanted to rise and kill Moses and Aaron for their predicament and said,

> *The land we passed through and explored is exceedingly good. If the Lord is pleased with us, he will lead us into that land, a land flowing with milk and honey, and will give it to us. Only do not rebel against the Lord. And do not be afraid of the people of the land, because we will de-*

vour them. Their protection is gone, but the Lord is with us. Do not be afraid of them."

(Numbers 14:7-9)

This is the same situation experienced by all the spies, but two different perspectives. One forgets the God who has brought them out of one trial after another; instead, rather believe the Canaanites are more powerful because they forgot that they wouldn't be fighting them on their strength or by themselves. While Joshua and Caleb knew that there's no way that their God can be defeated by the Canaanites, no matter if they're giants behind a fortified city. They understood nothing could come against them as long as their God is with them.

We need to remember that we must not be dismayed by whatever challenges we face because our God isn't like any other god. "If He's for us, who or what can come against us?" Fortunate for Joshua and Caleb, their faithfulness to our God who is worthy of our trust and faithfulness rewarded them the ability to possess the promised land while all their counterparts and everyone who doubted God was condemned to wander in the desert for a total of forty years, never to possess the land that God promised their ancestors.

This is significant for us to remember because our perspective can become our stumbling block if we're not aware. It can be the very thing that prevents us from being victorious. What does victorious mean? Victory can mean many things, but as we established, the victory we seek is to make God's name great and simply experience the grace, mercy, and favor from our obedience. The Israelites thought their primary goal was to possess the land flowing of milk and honey, not knowing that the promised land's inheritance was a byproduct of a much bigger plan. The ownership of the Promised Land would be a result of favor of their obedience. Whether they realized it or not, the real goal was to make God's name great among the nations. "The Master's Plan," has always been to make His name great and make Himself known among the nations so many can experience true freedom and healing that only could come from Him. Every challenge that God rescued them from allowed others to know and hear about a God who fights for them and will go to great lengths to rescue and protect them. As long as they know that they have a God fighting for them, He will save them from the hands of Pharaoh. He will continue to be a pillar of fire by night and a pillar of cloud by day. The same holds true for us today. He will empower us to slay our Goliath with a rock and a slingshot. He will empower us to move mountains in our lives that seem impossible to climb. There's always a caveat: we MUST remember who we serve and who we belong to as long as we remember to worship the One True God and forsake all counterfeit representations. Repeatedly, God reminds the Israelites to remember how He has met them at every turn and not to forget. Somehow, we're prone to amnesia. We know who to go to when we require rescue and forget just as quickly. As long as they remembered who fought for them and who they belonged to, they found success wherever they went. The minute they forgot that it was the I AM God who was the source of their victory, the source of their rescue, they experienced the separation from God and lost favor.

In the book of Joshua, we see evidence of their victory and defeat against their enemies. God promises Joshua success wherever he goes with a caveat.

> *Be strong and very courageous. Be careful to obey all the law my servant Moses gave you; do not turn from it to the right or to the left, that you may be successful wherever you go. Keep this Book of the Law always on your lips; meditate on it day and night, so that you may be careful to do everything written in it. Then you will be prosperous and successful. Have I not commanded you? Be strong and courageous. Do not be afraid; do not be discouraged, for the Lord your God will be with you wherever you go.*
>
> (Joshua 1:7-9 NIV)

Let's see what the cause of their victory was to the promised land. The limitless mindset is one where you keep your eye fixed on Jesus rather than the impossibility of your situation. The possibilities are limitless when God is in it. However, our brain seeks to protect us and tell us there's no way you can do it, and you fill in the blank. Your brain would be half right. Yes, you can't do it. Oh, you may have a certain amount of success doing it on your own, but we don't want a mediocre outcome. We want an outcome that defies human understanding. One in which you can't take the glory because it won't make sense in the earthly realm. We want an outcome that puts God's glory on display. Where nonbelievers say, "surely their God is The God." You can't do a God-sized plan on your own strength, but you can when God is in it.

In the first chapter of the Book of Joshua, God tells Joshua that he will carry on the mantle of Moses. He will be the one to lead the Israelites to the promised land. I wonder what Joshua was thinking! Who me? You want me to carry on where Moses left off? And if he thought this way, which scripture doesn't support that he thought this way, but we tend to think this way. Too many times, I thought this way! It became about me and my capabilities. And I forget it's not about me. It was never about Moses. Moses was the vessel in which God used to carry out His purposes, and we tend to want to give Moses credit, but God is the One. He was the One all along. We see that Joshua has quite a different conversation from what Moses had with God when God was calling him to something greater than himself.

Joshua didn't say, "Oh God, there's no way!" or "God, I'm not ready!" He accepted his assignment and acted. However, something powerful occurred to Joshua that cannot be missed, and it's what I call "the secret sauce." The power of the Holy Spirit working in us. In Deuteronomy 34:9 we see Joshua is filled with the Spirit. *"Now Joshua son of Nun was filled with the spirit of wisdom because Moses had laid his hands on him. So the Israelites listened to him and did what the Lord had commanded Moses" (Deuteronomy 34:9 NIV).*

When the Spirit of God rests on His people, the Holy Spirit enables us to move and speak powerfully and boldly because, at that point, we're allowing ourselves to be God's vessels. We're allowing our agenda to take a backseat. The agenda that we think are so great in our minds will never compare to God's plan. Paul said it best,

> *Now to Him who is able to do exceedingly abundantly above all that we ask or think, according to the power that works in us, to Him be glory in the church by Christ Jesus to all generations, forever and ever. Amen."*
>
> (Ephesians 3:20-21 NKJV)

Moses allowed his agenda to live a quiet life tending his flock to take a back seat, and God's agenda took center stage. Therefore, God exalted Moses as one of

God's representatives in the eyes of the Israelites and Pharaoh. Moses never took credit, and proof of that is seen in Rahab's response to the two the spies who secretly came to Jericho

> *I know that the Lord has given you this land and that a great fear of you has fallen on us, so that all who live in this country are melting in fear because of you. We have heard how the Lord dried up the water of the Red Sea for you when you came out of Egypt, and what you did to Sihon and Og, the two kings of the Amorites east of the Jordan, whom you completely destroyed. When we heard of it, our hearts melted in fear and everyone's courage failed because of you, for the Lord your God is God in heaven above and on the earth below.*
>
> (Joshua 2:8-11 NIV)

After decades from the time Moses led the Israelites out of Egypt, she responded rightly by saying, *"the Lord your God is God in heaven above and on the earth below."* Moses' obedience made God known in the Israelites' eyes and all the other nations that followed after other gods. Moses' obedience glorified God. To Rahab's credit, she had the wisdom to know that their God is indeed The God. And she was rewarded by being mentioned in the ancestral lineage of Jesus. Moses' impact reverberates still today. God equipped Moses with what he needed, which was Aaron, who "happens" (I believe a divine appointment) to be on his way to meet Moses to accompany and assist Moses. Then God took what Moses already possessed in his hand, which was his shepherd's staff. In some bible translations they refer to the staff as a rod.

> *"Then the Lord said to him, "What is that in your hand?" "A staff," he replied.*
> *The Lord said, "Throw it on the ground."*
> *Moses threw it on the ground and it became a snake, and he ran from it. 4 Then the Lord said to him, "Reach out your hand and take it by the tail." So Moses reached out and took hold of the snake and it turned back into a staff in his hand."*
>
> (Exodus 4:2-4 NIV)

This is one of many instances where the staff in Moses and Aaron's hand transformed into what they needed when they needed it. Aaron's staff transformed into a serpent in Aaron's hand and swallowed up the magicians' staff. On two separate occasions, Moses and Aaron's staff turned water into blood in the presence of Pharaoh. The staff in Aaron's hand caused frogs to cover the whole land, the staff in Moses' hand helped them defeat the Amalekites, and the staff was used to part the Red Sea. This is some of the many ways God used what was already in Moses' possession and transformed it into something more than Moses and Aaron could ever think or imagine.

STEPS OF FAITH

- What's "the staff" in your possession that at first sight seems insignificant or nothing especially spectacular? Write it down.
- Then, ask God to transform what you have into the miraculous.
- Ask God to provide you with what you need when you need it.

At each juncture of the journey, God guided Moses toward victory by equipping him with Aaron's partnership, transforming what he had and, most importantly, never leaving Moses' side. God was with Moses in the battle of wills with Pharoah. He was with Moses when the Egyptians sought to recapture the Israelites. He was with Moses as a pillar of fire by night and a pillar of cloud by day. God was with Moses when the people cried out for food. He provided food in the desert that fed thousands. This is our God whom you can trust to equip you, transform you to meet every challenge, and provide what you need when you need it. Will it be easy? Absolutely not, but you won't do it alone. If you invite Him every step of the way and establish a listening ear to hear the Holy Spirit. After all, the Holy

Spirit wants to teach you, guide you, empower you, and so much more.

Joshua's experience with God was no different from Moses. God makes a promise to Joshua, *"Just as I was with Moses so that I will be with you. I will not leave you or forsake you. Be strong and courageous, for you shall cause this people to inherit the land that I swore to their fathers to give them" (Joshua 1:5-6 ESV).* God directed him at every juncture. He equipped, transformed, and never left Joshua's side, guiding him along the way.

We see God positions Joshua well to gain the complete support of the people he will lead to the promised land,

> *Then they answered Joshua, "Whatever you have commanded us we will do, and wherever you send us we will go. Just as we fully obeyed Moses, so we will obey you. Only may the Lord your God be with you as he was with Moses. Whoever rebels against your word and does not obey it, whatever you may command them, will be put to death. Only be strong and courageous!"*
>
> (Joshua 1:16-18 NIV)

God will position you well for your assignment long before you're called. Moses was positioned in the palace well before it would be clear to him that he would return to the home he fled to lead his people of origin out, and Joshua was being groomed as Moses' aide to one day carry out what Moses started.

STEPS OF FAITH

- Only in retrospect can we see how God has positioned us for such a time as this. Where has God positioned you in your journey?
- How does it feel knowing that God is always with you? I hope it fosters more faith and greater belief when challenges arise.

In the first chapter of Joshua, God repeatedly encourages Joshua to "don't be afraid, be strong and courageous" like a parent encouraging their child to ride their bike for the first time..."You can do it! Mommy and Daddy are right here! Don't be afraid! You Got this!" I want you to know that God assured Moses and Aaron, and so many before and after them, that He would be with them every step of the way provided they remained faithful. The same holds true today. We serve a God who is true to His word. He doesn't play favorites. He will never "leave us or forsake us." that's why Jesus assured us that when He leaves, He will send us a Comforter, Holy Spirit to be with us in our wakings and our sleeping to guide us, lead us, teach us, empower us, give us wisdom, give us discernment, boldness, and so much more. So, take each step, whether you're afraid or nervous. The unknown tends to reveal doubt in our abilities, but I hope that doubt, fear, and anxiety will dissipate more so that unshakeable, immovable faith and belief take their place. Remember, "when God is in it, there is no limit."

You're made with purpose for a purpose!

PART IX

PLAN:

You will decide on a matter, and it will be established for you, and light will shine on your ways.

Job 22: 28

CHART YOUR DESTINATION

Define and Declare what's not a reality today, but possible tomorrow.

The old adage, "If you fail to plan, plan to fail" is why it's imperative we chart our destination with God. Who wants to fail at anything they start, then why start? Anything we plant, we're going to expect a harvest. Everything GOD does is to bring about a favorable outcome out of the darkness.

Psalm 127:1-2 (NIV)
Unless the Lord builds the house,
the builders labor in vain.
Unless the Lord watches over the city,
the guards stand watch in vain.
In vain you rise early
and stay up late,
toiling for food to eat—
for he grants sleep to those he loves.

> *1 Cor. 15:58*
> *"Therefore, my beloved brethren, be steadfast, immovable, always abounding in the work of the Lord, knowing that your toil is not in vain in the Lord." NKJV*

> *Haggai 1: 6 (NKJV)*
> *"You have sown much, and bring in little;*
> *You eat, but do not have enough;*
> *You drink, but you are not filled with drink;*
> *You clothe yourselves, but no one is warm;*
> *And he who earns wages,*
> *Earns wages to put into a bag with holes."*

God doesn't do anything without expecting a favorable return. He healed, expecting healing. He multiplied five loaves and three fish expecting to feed thousands. He turned water to wine at the wedding celebration expecting to have more than enough. That's who our God is! He is more than enough! He is more than enough for whatever we carry or come up against. The key is not wanting to do anything without Him. Attempting to do it without Him will always put us at a deficit. His word says apart from Him we cannot do anything.

Our God is a God of abundance. Revisit Genesis and see how He prepared the dwelling place for his prize possession, humankind; His children. This dwelling place lacked nothing. It had everything and then some. It had so many trees, so many herbs, so many kinds of sea creatures, land creatures, and flying creatures. That's our God! We, after all, are made in THEIR likeness. But what I quickly learned is that we're made for His good pleasure. Therefore, if we pursue the things that will bring Him good pleasure, we'll inevitably experience pleasure. Have you ever heard or met people who enjoy their work: even though it took time and energy, it didn't feel like work? They don't grow tired of it because they believe this is what they were made to do. They can't wait to do it, and they can spend hours devoted to it. I'm hoping we can live more in that space.

I remember many years of pursuing acting, which is a calling not designed for the weak. It's countless hours perfecting your craft, pounding on doors, enduring hunger, experiencing rejection in hopes of the moment when all the sacrifice pays off. You get that role or take part in a project that sets your soul on fire. You would have to love it and be willing to go through all the hills and valleys this profession promises to offer. Your ministry, your mission that was already prepared for you, will have to be what you were made to do in order to sustain you for the long haul when you want to throw in the towel. The only thing that will prevent you from doing so will be that inner pull, the Holy Spirit within that won't allow you to stop.

I wonder if Martin Luther King Jr. had any moments when he wanted to throw in the towel and live his life without the weight of the world on his shoulders or this burden for justice. He knew death was possible and, at one point, inevitable. His "I've Been to the Mountaintop" speech, given on April 3, 1968, at Bishop Charles Mason Temple, Memphis, Tennessee, alluded to his understanding and surrender that he may very well not see the fruit of his labor, but he was at peace with that. Why? I imagine he knew his purpose was far greater than he was. While he had worldwide recognition and fame, it seemed he had an understanding; it wasn't about him.

We need to remember while the outcome may garner us success, fame, and even financial wealth. The result isn't the goal but merely a gift from the One, who gives and provides abundance. This is where the trap lies when we pursue the outcome and not the purpose, and we wonder why we feel unfulfilled and bored because we forgot that we're made for God's pleasure and not the other way around where we're demanding God to fulfill our pleasures and desires. Don't think that God isn't interested in our desires for a car or house. Again, God loves to bless. He prefers to bless instead of handing out judgment. After all, Jesus is delaying his return so that none will perish. He wants as many of His creations to dwell with Him in the new earth and the new heaven. Read Revelation 21 to get a glimpse of the beauty and majesty that God is planning for His children; it won't be shabby or dreary. The colors will be so vivid they won't compare to anything we've seen. That's our God!

PART IX

I'm reminded of David and Solomon in the Old Testament; both had a heart for God. Their faith and desire to please God were authentic and well placed, but when the blessings and favor poured out, they began to lose their focus. Their focus that was once on God slowly shifted to other desires. They didn't even realize and notice when it was happening? I wonder if they could pinpoint the moment when their gaze shifted from God to the worship, admiration, and approval of man. Well, my friend, just like it could happen to them, it can indeed happen to us. We want to put guard rails in place to prevent that very thing from happening. I can remember my fellow actors making statements that they won't change when they make it big; they won't forget where they came from and yada, yada. I'm sure they believed what they said and meant it with all sincerity, but it's a naive thing to say. How can you not be changed if you reach a level of recognition and status? You must change; change is good, and there's nothing wrong with change. Hopefully, the change you're experiencing makes you wiser and bolder. Hopefully, the change that's occurring within reminds you of what the goal is, rather than the outcome of laboring in the fields. We want to experience a harvest. If you don't desire a harvest, then what's the purpose of planting seeds and laboring? God wants a return on His investment. Remember, you won't be doing this in your own power, but the power of The One who will empower you, the

Holy Spirit. This is evident in the parable of the talents. God expected a return. He was pleased with the ones who multiplied what they received and displeased with the ones who did nothing. We see Jesus multiplying five loaves and two fish. Also, the water into wine at the wedding. God is limitless! God doesn't know any other way to operate. These are the lenses that our God sees, so His children must know and see the way He sees. I want you to embrace the fact that God will bless your efforts, provided you're planting His seeds. Why wouldn't He want His seeds to bear fruit? In Mark 11:12-14,20-21 and Matthew 21: 18-22, Jesus cursed the fig tree that provided no figs because He deemed it useless; it served no purpose if it wouldn't do what it was created to do. We don't want to be deemed useless. I know I don't! I'll venture to say you don't want to either. We want to serve the purpose for which we were uniquely created. Remember, God had already prepared a work for us to do way in advance before we knew it was assigned for us to do. In both accounts, the fig tree withered from the roots, never to bear fruit again, but Jesus goes on to say in both accounts to have faith. We are going to need this kind of faith that's described in Matthew to pursue the God-sized purpose given to us.

> *"Have faith in God," Jesus answered. "Truly I tell you, if anyone says to this mountain, 'Go, throw yourself into the sea,' and do not doubt in their heart but believe that what*

they say will happen, it will be done for them. Therefore, I tell you, whatever you ask for in prayer, believe that you have received it, and it will be yours. And when you stand praying, if you hold anything against anyone, forgive them, so that your Father in heaven may forgive you your sins."

(Mark 11: 22-25 NIV)

This scripture seems straightforward, but we tend to be challenged with "whatever you ask for in prayer, believe that you received it, and it will be yours." We'll need to have this unwavering faith as we chart this journey toward our purpose. However, what do we do when we don't receive what "we ask in prayer, believing that we received it"? This is the conundrum. Do we stop asking and believing that we have received it before we have actually received it? If we're honest, we tend to believe loosely, so we minimize disappointment if we don't receive what we asked for. I remember when well-meaning Christians would say you didn't receive your prayer request because of doubt, didn't have strong enough faith, or maybe unforgiveness is the culprit. This is the worst thing we, as Christians, can do with this scripture. I remember when I prayed for my mom's healing, and God chose not to grant that prayer. In my immature faith, I found myself no longer praying or believing. I thought to myself, what's the use in praying or believing in the impossible. God will make His decision, regardless of what I do. Yet, God invites us into a relationship with Him in prayer that He desires us to be rooted in trust, hope, belief in Him, and unwavering faith that He can do the impossible. Whether God grants us our request, He desires our belief and faith to be unwavering. I think we want to be sure to don't miss Jesus' first words, "Have faith in God," we want to make sure our "faith" is in God's Sovereignty and NOT our prayers to Him.

I'm astonished that at the peak of Martin Luther King Jr.'s purpose, he was in his mid-twenties. He died at the age of thirty-nine. Martin was a young man, but He seemed wise beyond his years. I get the sense he communed with God so much, so he was clear about what he was made for, and he surrendered to it at all costs. I wonder if his wife ever resented his unwavering commitment to the call on his life. If I were his wife, I might have encouraged him to abandon this road and take the safe and normal road. Who would blame her! I suspect "normal," whatever that means, wasn't an option for him. It would mean complacency, stagnation, and, most of all, disobedience. Or is safe and normal, fine by you? Hey, I think you need to know yourself. That was the whole reason why we spent so much time revisiting our history, identifying our strengths and weaknesses so that we can embark on this journey sober-minded. Jesus surrendered with full awareness of what it was going to cost. He wasn't caught off guard. He understood His purpose. He asked God, the Father, to allow this cup to pass, but He quickly said, not my will but yours be done. Are you ready to surrender to the purpose on your life at all costs? Are you prepared to say not my will God, but yours? Are you ready?

At one time, I considered writing a book to guide parents to get their kids into the entertainment industry. My kids were in the entertainment industry, and parents would mention how they want to get their kids into acting. I would often get approached on how to start. They wanted guidance, so I thought I would write this book from a parent's perspective. There weren't a lot of books out there to help parents navigate this tricky road. I saw dollar signs and felt confident to write this book. After all, it was what I knew. Then, I sensed the Holy Spirit's prompting that that wasn't the book I was to write. I wasn't to write that book, but the one you're holding in your hand.

I questioned God's prompting. I know I shouldn't have questioned, but I did. I knew more about how to navigate minors within the entertainment industry. It made the most sense, right? Write what you know, right? However, I knew, without question, this was a prompting from God. I didn't want to do it. It was a scary thought. I felt foolish even. *Who am I?* I thought, *how am I going to lead someone to their purpose?* There are countless books out there to inspire you toward your purpose. The notion of writing such a book was scary and daunting. Yet, I couldn't shake off this prompting to do it. I quickly knew it would require me to surrender my ego and others' thoughts, desires, and imposed expectations and commit to being vulnerable and sharing what's given to me by the Holy Spirit and my journey. When I forced my own agenda, writing became arduous, but the moment I let the Holy Spirit, along with prayer, lead my writing, it became more joyful and less tedious.

I've concluded that when you surrender to the purpose God has predestined for you, it will come at a cost: your time, popularity, comfort, and, dare I say, maybe the life you envisioned for yourself. That was evident with Martin Luther King Jr. and Moses. Moses was at Midian for years living a comfortable life devoid of stress when confronted with his purpose that was already prepared for him when he was floating down the Nile River as a baby. He traded safe and easy for unsafe and difficult, trying to convince Pharaoh to do the right thing. Have you ever tried to convince someone of something to no avail? It's not fun! My personality would quickly cause me to give up, trying to change anyone's mind. He traded his safety and normality to lead Israelites who wanted to kill him and criticized him throughout the journey. However, Joseph didn't have a complete choice on the series of events that would unfold in his life. He knew he had a purpose that was revealed to him in a dream as a young boy. I wonder if that dream sustained him when everything around him was contrary to the dream given to him. I wonder if that dream was God's kindness toward him to remain faithful when he found himself thrown into the well by his brothers, sold as a slave, then sentenced to jail. Did the dream that revealed to him that he was destined for greatness sustain him when Potiphar's wife tried to seduce him. I suspect his relationship with God prevented him from abandoning his moral compass and sleep with Potiphar's wife. I'm sure if he did sleep with her, she probably would have made life in Egypt bearable for him.

However, he was willing to remain firm in who he was created and remain faithful to God's precepts. God ultimately blessed him a hundredfold. Joseph rose to the second in command. I can't find anywhere in scripture where he let his power as Egypt's second in command overtake his moral compass. He was positioned not only for his own gain. Although he received a blessing by way of position, stature, and wealth, he was positioned for the sole purpose to rescue the Israelites from the famine that was the true purpose of his elevation to the position of Egypt's number two. However, we confuse the position as the goal rather than the purpose, which had to do more about the Israelites than his personal gain. Joseph's gain was merely a byproduct of his continued obedience.

STEPS OF FAITH

- Where did God open doors of opportunity that simply wasn't about you but a larger purpose beyond you? If you can't recall these opportunities, I encourage you to start looking for them.

I love God's patience with Peter, which should give us hope. While Peter took his eye off the goal for a moment, God didn't discard him. He was determined to restore Peter for the calling that he was already predestined. John the Baptist knew in the womb what he was predestined to do when he leapt in his mother's womb when Jesus, his cousin, was in the womb of Mary. He was to make the way ready for the One he was unworthy to tie His sandals. Can you imagine his role to tell people that they need to repent when they don't want to? Paul, who was hunting Christians to persecute, was now being the one persecuted. He could have remained in his previous role of power and influence safe from persecution, but he couldn't ignore what was made so clear to him. I could go on and on.

STEPS OF FAITH

- What has God made clear to you?
- How has He positioned you?

PART IX

Now that we're clear. We want to take what we know to be true in the spiritual realm and give it legs and feet in the natural realm. We'll create a tangible plan that will help us bring this from a knowing to a reality that can benefit others because our gifts and talents aren't for our own gain but others' benefit. If this book were for me just to say I'm an author and not for the encouragement and benefit of those who will read it, then it might as well be like that fig tree bearing no fruit, deemed useless. There are enough books out there. Why one more? Why this one?

My prayer is that this book will remove the shackles from those who doubt their abilities, feel it's too late, feel foolish to pursue their purpose, or don't know where to start or how to start. Whatever prevented you from getting out of the safe boat and venture to walk on water toward Jesus, I hope and pray that you come away feeling encouraged and empowered by the Holy Spirit. But I don't only want to leave you encouraged and empowered like so many books. There's nothing wrong with that. However, I know the best-laid plans die with excitement and encouragement. You need more to get you over the threshold.

You need a plan that will help you eat ALL of the elephant in small bites. I'm sure you've heard this analogy. I never knew why you would want to eat an elephant, but I suspect the enormity of the elephant could make it feel that it's impossible. However, if you consistently eat the elephant in small bite-size pieces, you'll eventually consume all of it. The obstacle we'll have to overcome is our frustration at the speed at which we eat the elephant or if the elephant could be eaten at all. We need to shift our focus from the enormity of the elephant and focus on chewing the elephant steadily and consistently. We do that, and there will surely be a carcass. We want to leave nothing unfinished. We want to finish what we start. We want to be determined to finish what we start. And we will!

Desire vs. Commitment

I had a coach give an analogy between desire and commitment. We desire to learn another language and travel the world, but we're committed to protecting our child from harm's way. We're committed to keeping that toddler from going into the street. It's not a mere desire but a full-fledged commitment.

STEPS OF FAITH

- What are you committed to accomplishing?
- What's that giant-sized goal you're committed to devoting your life to at the cost of your personal desires?
- Write down milestones and achievable actionable steps with a timeline.

PART IX

Your Reason

When you have a compelling reason to reach your giant-sized goal, it could be the difference between success and failure. For me, the why of this goal seems evident. I don't want to take my last breath without accomplishing the things I was created to do. I want you to get even clearer about your why. Write it down.

STEPS OF FAITH

- Why is it imperative you pursue this giant-sized God goal?
- Who will benefit from your commitment? If Jesus hadn't been committed to His calling, I shudder to think where we would be.

A dear sister-friend of mine, Sarah Dornbos, surrendered to the purpose to develop Kids Hope, an after-school mentoring program designed to encourage and support youth who may fall through the educational system's cracks without this added support. She didn't set out saying this is what I wanted to do for my life, but a series of events made it clear to her that this was what she was called to do. Since accepting the call, countless families and kids have had their lives changed forever. Can you imagine the countless lives that wouldn't have experienced the impact of this program? Also, the lives of the mentors have changed. They receive something too in their giving. I can think of countless organizations that I've supported either financially or in service to, such as Dressember, Treasures, and the Living Room. They're thriving organizations that had small beginnings. I wonder as they were taking their first bite of the elephant, could they have imagined the scope of their impact on the lives of many. I don't want to consider the lives that wouldn't have experienced their impact had they not got out of the boat in faith and walked toward Jesus.

STEPS OF FAITH

- Where do you need to get out of the safe boat in faith to walk toward Jesus? Jesus who promises never to leave you or forsake you.
- Do you believe that He will never leave you or forsake you?

Well, I want you to know God never left Moses, Joseph, Paul, Mary, Jesus, etc. Even when God seemed like he was nowhere to be found, he was there. He was always there. Remind yourself of that. You'll have to remind yourself of that continually. God always told the Israelites to do something in remembrance or reminded them to remember when he was there. Why? Because God knows we need reminding. We have a short-term memory. That's why it's so important to be in God's Word to remind yourself of who you are and who He is. When the going gets tough, and you want to raise the white flag, remember who's in your corner! Remember who fights for you! Remember, there's The One who has devised a plan that's intended for your good. If you only focus on Jesus' crucifixion, you could think how his blood-soaked body on that cross is for His good or mine. And it was, He is seated on the right hand of the Father, and He will return surrounded by clouds, not like a sacrificial lamb, but a powerful lion in all of His majesty and power. His crucified body seems like the end of His story, but scriptures assure us it's not. He is resurrected, defeating death, and seated on the right hand of the Father to reign forever.

STEPS OF FAITH

- Define and declare your Giant-Sized God Purpose Commitment
- Be clear on your why? Who will benefit from your commitment? This will be your why?

Hopefully, your reason is compelling enough to fuel you when things get too hard. Frequently, it's not that it's hard or impossible, but we're being taken out of our comfort zone, which makes it feel hard.

Now, I want you to brainstorm what it will take to get from point A to point B. Think of it as your GPS. The acronym for GPS is the Global Positioning System. All I know is that I'm beyond thankful for the GPS. I remember the days when I had to take my Thomas Guide out. I know, I'm dating myself. We then graduated to printing out the directions on our desktop computer ahead of time, but good luck if you got rerouted for construction or some other unforeseen mishap. You were screwed. One of the best features of smartphones is being able to use them as our navigation device. I'm thankful my phone will tell me when I missed my turn and attempt to reroute me if I choose to listen.

Well, the GPS is only as effective if you input a starting location and your final destination. Otherwise, it's of no use. Without either information, it will be hard to move forward. So, we'll start with the end in mind and work backward, simply like making your favorite meal. First, we have to identify what cuisine we're in the mood for. Once we've done that, now we can identify the dishes that are reflective of that particular cuisine. Let's say we're in the mood for soul food. Once we have established the cuisine, we can now select our menu. When you think of soul food, what comes to mind? I immediately think of fried catfish, baked macaroni and cheese, collard greens, cornbread, and a peach cobbler as the dessert. That sounds like a traditional soul-food meal. Now that I've set my menu, I can list all the ingredients needed to create these dishes. Then we have to know where we can buy these particular items. Does it require me to go to a specialty store? Thankfully, everything on the list can be found at the local grocery store. Now that I have all my ingredients, I'll need to know what ingredient needs to be handled first and how. Will it require kneading, whisking, tenderizing, marinated, blending, chopping? Then I must identify how this meal must be prepared. Are we chilling it in the refrigerator or freezer, baked, grilled, braised, fried, or sauteed? Do you consume immediately, or does it need to rest for a certain amount of time before it can be consumed? How does it need to be consumed with chopsticks, spoon, knife, and fork or good old-fashioned fingers? After that's thought out and executed, then and only then can you consume what you've made.

You need to step back at this Giant-Sized God Purpose, figure out what you'll need, what you need to learn, who you'll need to enlist or hire to help. You want to get so specific that you're not missing any of the necessary ingredients like the yeast to cause your bread to rise. Bread isn't bread if there's no yeast to cause it to rise. Take your time and do as much homework as possible to ensure a successful outcome. However, I want to also caution you that there may not be a recipe for what you're called to make, and that's when you must have a prayer life that's connected to the Holy Spirit to empower you, guide you, teach you, lead you, and so much more. Remember, God is the one who has deposited this desire in your heart, so He will equip you. Just like He equipped Moses, Joseph, Mary, and Jesus. God won't call you to something and abandon you and say good luck, "peace out!" That's why we want to be more sure than not; God leads us to this journey and not our desires and ego. I loved when Moses said to God in Exodus that if He won't be with him, he doesn't want to go. I've prayed that same prayer. I don't want to go or take one more step forward without knowing He will be with me. I know for sure I'll be victorious if He is with me, whatever the outcome. Without Him, without His covering, I shudder at the thought of what the journey and outcome would be. So, my admonition is to pray every step of the way. Cultivate a life of prayer. Cultivate a habit of prayer. I'm reminded that whenever Moses and Aaron experience opposition, they lay face down prostrate in prayer. They didn't spend a lot of time engaging in arguments, planning, or deep discussion. They got down to business and prayed. Jesus did the same thing. The Bible mentions countless times that Jesus snuck away to pray. He needed to sneak away to pray to get replenishment, direction, and discernment. He had to do that. He was always pouring out to his disciples and those who needed healing and correction. He needed to sneak away to pray and replenish and commune with His Father in heaven to be sure He is doing what Father tells Him. He knew it was imperative to pray because He was about to FINISH the very thing He was sent to do in the form of a man, a baby born to Mary. Just before His crucifixion, He went away to pray and fast.

Fasting

Fasting was most necessary for Him to do because He was going to be tempted by the enemy, the father of lies. I think it was significant to fast to withstand the enemy in the flesh. There's something about surrendering your fleshly desires. My experience of fasting is that the first few days are the most difficult. You want that thing your flesh says you need, says it must have. After a few days, you start to desire less and less of the thing you were craving. You begin not to yearn for it. You start to understand that you can do without it longer than you thought. I've intentionally made it vague about what to fast because it doesn't always have to be food. It could be talking, TV, shopping, smoking, etc. I recommend you pray about what you're abstaining from. Ask God what seems to have your attention that should be reserved for Him. Usually, whatever has your attention or seems impossible to give up is the very thing you should give up.

There's a gift in incorporating fasting as part of your prayer life. The bible has countless accounts when God's people fast, and Jesus himself fast. Why is fasting necessary? Why is it useful? Why should I incorporate this practice? As I mentioned above, Jesus fasted in the garden. Jesus modeled a life He desires us to live. There's a gift available to us when we incorporate fasting as a practice. We can gain clarity in a situation, and we can hear God more clearly as we remove distractions.

STEPS OF FAITH

- Who or what has your desire and your attention that should be reserved for God?
- Ask the Holy Spirit to guide you in your fast. If fasting from food, always seek medical counsel and begin slowly. Perhaps with fasting from one meal, then from sunrise to sunset. Define your purposes and duration. Search scriptures to understand when and why fasting was implemented. Let the scriptures be your guide.

Our God is a jealous God! He desires all our adoration, worship, and praise. We'll establish some practices that will help us develop an intimate relationship with God and destroy the plans of the enemy. When the disciples asked Jesus why they couldn't heal the man possessed by demons, Jesus replied this kind requires praying and fasting. When you're contending with the enemy, it will require prayer and fasting. After all, his sole purpose is to kill, steal, and destroy the good plans for your life. He'll use all kinds of tactics to accomplish his assignment. Who will complete their assignment first? The devil or you? I hope it's you. I hope you won't get distracted. I hope you won't procrastinate. I hope you won't give up. I hope you won't allow doubts and lies spoken over you as a child to seem more real than what God has said about you. This is why you spent time revisiting your past traumas and experiences, so they won't threaten to sabotage the plans God has for you and what He wants to do through you. You'll need a running partner and a team to ensure you make it to the finish line, but before we delve into what your team should be designed to do, I want to bring to your attention some tools necessary to run the race that's set before you.

Worship

I don't know about you, but music, specifically worshipping in song, always shifts my heart when I need it the most. I heard it said it's difficult to worship and be angry at the same time. When I feel discouraged, the right worship song can empower me to cling to hope again. Something happens when you allow yourself to worship in song with all that's in you. I say worship is like praying twice. There's a reason why almost every faith denomination includes music in its service. For the Christian faith, worship always precedes the sermon. It's intentional; it ushers you into the presence of the Lord. You can get out of your head and let your heart be moved and open to receive. This may seem silly, but I want to encourage you to find a song or songs that will pick up your spirit and remind you of the God who is with you. You'll need reminding, so choose well.

STEPS OF FAITH

- Write down the anthem song that will encourage you to carry on when you feel discouraged, fearful, or unsure of your abilities.

Devotional and Meditation

Many worthy devotionals can assist you to commune with God. The purpose of devotionals is to develop a consistent practice of meditating on God's Word, therefore communing with the One who created you. However, your Bible should serve as your primary devotional. Suppose you're not sure how to use your Bible in this way. Most people start in the Psalms; however, ask the Holy Spirit to direct you to a book or a passage of scripture that will ground your time with the Lord. Carve out uninterrupted quiet time to immerse yourself in God's Word. Depending on the scripture, utilize all your senses. Transport yourself in the story or put yourself in the shoes of the person mentioned in the scripture. I recently discovered the practice of singing scripture and not just the Psalms. We want to chew on His Word. "In the beginning was the Word, and the Word was with God, and Word was God" (John 1:1 NIV). After all, this is an opportunity to develop intimacy with God, whom you'll need to direct your every step as you put hands and feet to the purpose He planted in your heart.

STEPS OF FAITH

- Decide how you're going to engage with God's Word daily and write it down. It doesn't have to be the same every day. However, if you're new to engaging with God's Word, I recommend establishing a practice of being in God's Word first that's manageable for you and then explore other ways of engaging in God's Word. Start by blocking out time in your calendar. If you're not intentional about setting a time, the demands of this world take priority.
- Grab your calendar. Guard your time with God by placing it in the books. I have an appointment on this day_____ at this time _____. Doing this will ensure your time with God won't fall to the wayside or become an afterthought. The goal is to have your time with God become

the norm and not the exception. I prefer to have my time with God to start my day. It centers me and I won't let curveballs of the day hijack my day to the point that I'm left empty and too tired to engage with God.

Prayer

You need clarity when you pray. You want to be specific. Let's begin by asking ourselves some poignant questions. What are you praying for? Is your prayer life in alignment with God? There are so many books on prayer. How to pray, what to pray for, and so many other aspects of prayer. The disciples even asked Jesus to teach them how to pray. They acknowledged that His prayer life was distinctively different than what they were accustomed to or have experienced. In Matthew 6: 9-13, Jesus offers a blueprint to praying to the Almighty God. These are some of my takeaways:

1. Acknowledgement of his Sovereignty and Holiness
2. Surrender to His will and plan
3. Our request for our daily needs
4. Repentant heart extending mercy as we desire mercy
5. Assurance that He will deliver us from the snares of the enemy

6. The promise we'll dwell in the House of the Lord forever.

Our God is most definitely concerned about our well-being. Proof of that's evident in Psalms 119:1. He turns His ears to the cries of His children. However, that's not only what concerns Him. My prayer is that we would grow in maturity in our prayer life that we begin to pray for the things that concern and grieve our Father's heart. This practice will also help us from being self-centered in our prayers. Scriptures say that Jesus goes to intercede in prayer for us and the Holy Spirit already knows what to pray concerning us. Mind-blowing, I know. Let that comfort you as you develop a mature prayer life.

STEPS OF FAITH

- Ask the Holy Spirit to help you have a heart for the things that grieve your Creator's heart. Write down what the Holy Spirit speaks to you. This exercise may take several times of asking before it's clear and becomes a daily practice.
- Now, I want you to incorporate scripture in your prayer life. There's nothing more powerful than recalling God's character and truth in prayer. Our words alone are hollow with-

out the power of God's spirit-filled Words. The next topic will help to apply this more easily.

Memorization

Whether memorization comes easy or not, it's a practice worth pursuing. I'm going to encourage you to memorize scripture. As I mentioned in previous chapters, you want to recall scripture when you need it most, just like Jesus did in the garden of Gethsemane when Satan was tempting him. He responded to each temptation with "It is written" and told Satan what "is written." When you're being attacked with doubt, fear, and insecurities, you need to be ready to douse the flames of lies with God's truth. And the only way I know of doing that's by having His Words on my lips ready to utter whether I'm communing with God or in battle with the adversary. Memorization will also help you incorporate them in your private prayer time.

STEPS OF FAITH

- Until this point, you've been directed to search scriptures that will remind you of who God says you are. Now, I want you to find scriptures that remind you of who God is so you can be reminded of who is in your corner and who resides in you.

Visualization

We are visual people. Some of us are visual learners. Our eyes can get us into trouble and get us distracted, very much like a dog trained to listen to its owner to avoid being distracted by other dogs. Still, it can also help us establish our environment and set a mood. I have many teachers as friends, and they always have to prepare their classrooms at the beginning of the school year. They intend to create an environment for learning, encouragement, and growth. I love entering a school where the kids' works are displayed on the walls, and words of encouragement adorn the walls. It leaves me with a sense of creativity, growth, and excitement for learning. Some Christians are opposed to a vision board for one reason or another. I recommend you create one that will encourage you and remind you of the vision God placed on your heart. God always gave His people a vision and direction. When He told His people to build the Ark of the Covenant, Noah's Ark and the Temple were spectacularly detailed, and I imagined visually appealing. Your vision board could be words, phrases, pictures, scriptures, outline, or media. Whatever you decide, this vision board is intended for your eyes. It's intended for you, so don't censor what it should look like for others' approval. It should move you, encourage you, and direct you.

STEPS OF FAITH

- Create a vision board that will affirm and remind you of the purpose that God has placed on your heart. Once you have created your board, make sure you have access to it when you need reminding, inspiration, or encouragement.

Celebrate and Feast

God loves to party! In the Old Testament, there are a bunch of Feasts mentioned. A feast for this and a feast for that. God created reasons to celebrate; read Leviticus if you need proof. In fact, the Feasts were holy. I want you to find times and ways to celebrate and know that it's a holy and sacred thing you're doing if you're anything like me. I can cross off one thing on my list, and I'm on to the next thing. I don't take nearly enough time to acknowledge or celebrate that I finished a bite of the elephant. We think we should only celebrate when the elephant is completely consumed. We rob ourselves of the fullness of the journey God wants to take us on. When the Israelites crossed over the Red Sea successfully, they celebrated with tambourines, singing, and dancing. They were praising God for His faithfulness. The celebration doesn't need to be big. It could be simply sharing with a loved one that will join you in your celebration of a milestone accomplished. It could be a reward for yourself. It could be just breaking out in dance by yourself or even worshipping God's goodness. Whatever it looks like or needs to be, make sure to carve out time for it. It will fuel you and encourage you.

Let's recap! Clarity breeds direction, and we saw that putting necessary information into our GPS will lead us to successfully arriving at our destination. We want to be clear on the mission, what we're committed to, and why.

You were made with purpose for a purpose!

PART X

ACCOUNTABILITY:

Brothers, join in imitating me, and keep your eyes on those who walk according to the example you have in us.

Philippians 3:17

CHOOSE YOUR RUNNING PARTNER

Accountability as a Gift

These days, people don't want to be held accountable to anyone for their actions. We want to set our standards of what it means to be responsible to one another. Yet scripture is always challenging us to hold one another accountable as a gift to one another, and we'll have to give an account to Him on judgment day. "So then, each of us will give an account of ourselves to God" (Romans 14:12 NIV). We have a responsibility to one another. In Genesis 4: 9, we witness a conversation between God and Cain. " Then the Lord said to Cain, "Where is Abel your brother?" He said, " I don't know; am I my brother's keeper?" In essence, he was saying I'm not responsible for his whereabouts or well-being; yet we know, and God knew he was very much responsible for his brother's whereabouts and demise. But before Cain's unfortunate choice, God says, in verses 8-9, "...sin is crouching at the door. Its desire is contrary to you, but you must rule over it." God was trying to warn

Cain of a blind spot that could lead him to destruction. However, Cain didn't heed God's warning, became a prisoner to his actions, and murdered his brother.

What are some ways we can ensure we don't get sideswiped by our unintended blind spots? We can begin by holding ourselves accountable, acknowledging we're accountable to God, which is a good thing. He is the best accountability partner a person can have because He wants us to succeed and not fail, so He is worthy of our trust and surrender. Then I recommend having at least one trusted person in your life with whom you can be fully transparent and can rely on to point out your blind spots lovingly. If you don't have close relationships for one reason or another, I suggest a counselor, therapist, or small recovery group. There are countless recovery and support groups that can serve as accountability partners of sorts. As I mentioned earlier in the book, I reaped the benefits of being part of a recovery group for a time. Suppose you're of that mindset that says, "That's not for me. I don't need a group or counseling!" I say, don't be quick to dismiss the healing and the gift that's available. There's an unexpected gift in allowing yourself to be accountable to someone.

Interestingly, practically every recovery and 12-step program that's not faith-based has embedded as part of their core practices implementing some form of accountability, whether it's showing up to a meeting consistently or choosing a partner as a sponsor. They have an innate knowing that there's a benefit in partnership and community. Either way, success is gained by being accountable to another person. One of my favorite scriptures to recite is, "Therefore, confess your sins to one another, and pray for one another so that you may be healed. The effective prayer of a righteous man can accomplish much" (James 5:16 NIV). I'm comforted that the intent of confessing and sharing the hard things of life is for the edification and healing of one another. This practice serves as a gift to one another if we choose to see it that way.

When I decided to make my reentry into the entertainment industry, I knew I would need key people in my inner circle to help me with any possible blind spots. I knew the entertainment industry is inherently filled with pitfalls that one could fall prey to, so I had to ensure I didn't fall prey to the lure of money and the temptations of fame and ambition, which could lead me to say yes to things that go against my core beliefs. Hence, I knew it would be necessary to partner with trusted individuals who could lovingly bring to my attention anything that might arise as a blind spot.

STEPS OF FAITH

- If you don't already have one or more persons who serve as your life accountability partners, I recommend you make a list of possible can-

didates. Choose wisely. Ask God to reveal who should occupy this role.
- Make a list of what you'll permit them to say or do, thereby setting a healthy communicated boundary as a protection for one another.
- Schedule a time to talk to them about the role you would like them to play in your life. It's essential to be clear of the expectations, so there's no confusion.

Strength in Numbers

According to a widely known African proverb, "If you want to go fast, walk alone. If you want to go far, go together." We want to go far in this God pursuit, which will require us to develop partnerships and, eventually, a team to allow us to go the distance.

I'm thankful for the partnership I have with my sisters, who were ordained by God, because I know they have my back without question. I'm thankful that God, in His wisdom, has given us one another in partnership to do life together. God ordained Moses and Aaron's relationship as brothers and united them to carry the work Moses was born to fulfill. Read how God partnered Moses and Aaron in Exodus Chapter 4 after Moses' hesitation to lead the Israelites out of Egypt. For the most part, their relationship always held as a united front, except in two instances where they were out of sync. The first instance was when Moses left Aaron in charge when he went to speak to God in the mountain only to find that Aaron allowed the Israelites to create graven images to worship, which is a "no no" by God standards, and when Miriam and Aaron opposed Moses in Numbers Chapter 12, which didn't fare well for the both of them. Aside from those two instances, they worked perfectly in unison and recovered from setbacks along the way. Your partnerships aren't going to be perfect, but hopefully, they're grounded in respect so that if situations arise, you both will be able to recover and move forward.

There's strength in numbers! Moses and Aaron had several cases in their assignment when they were stronger together, for instance, when they came before Pharaoh during the many plagues. Also, when the very people they were called to lead out of Egypt were prepared to kill them, they fell to the ground prostrate together in prayer. The key word there is "together." They encouraged and supported one another, which served the mission.

You want to choose your partnership wisely, whether it be temporary or long term. Whom you decide to partner with will be a reflection of you. This relationship can either propel you forward or bring confusion. In starting this journey, it may feel like a one-person show, and it may very well be for the moment, but as God increases your influence, and territory, you'll need the wisdom to know when it's time to enlist help and expand your team.

In Exodus Chapter 18, Moses' father-in-law, Jethro, pointed out a few blind spots for Moses when he visited him in the desert. And a good thing that he did!

> *The next day Moses sat to judge the people, and the people stood around Moses from morning till evening. When Moses' father-in-law saw all that he was doing for the people, he said, "What is this that you are doing for the people? Why do you sit alone, and all the people stand around you from morning till evening?" And Moses said to his father-in-law, "Because the people come to me to inquire of God; when they have a dispute, they come to me and I decide between one person and another, and I make them know the statutes of God and his laws." Moses' father-in-law said to him, "What you are doing is not good. You and the people with you will certainly wear yourselves out, for the thing is too heavy for you. You are not able to do it alone. Now obey my voice; I will give you advice, and God be with you! You shall represent the people before God and bring their cases to God, and you shall warn them about the statutes and the laws, and make them know the way in which they must walk and what they must do. Moreover, look for able men from all the people, men who fear God, who are trustworthy and hate a bribe, and place such men over the people as chiefs of thousands, of hundreds, of fifties, and of tens. And let them judge the people at all times.*

PART X

> *Every great matter they shall bring to you, but any small matter they shall decide themselves. So it will be easier for you, and they will bear the burden with you. If you do this, God will direct you, you will be able to endure, and all these people also will go to their place in peace.*
>
> (Exodus 18: 13-23 ESV)

It's ironic that this is the same Moses who once questioned and doubted his abilities with God at the burning bush to the Moses who believe he's the only one who can judge and teach the Israelites God's statutes. Thankfully for him, he had the sound and loving wisdom of his father-in-law to bring to his attention a blind spot that wouldn't serve him, the people, and his mission well. Jethro pointed out that it's not good for him to do this alone, or he'll wear himself out and that this is a burden that's too heavy for him to carry alone. While Moses didn't enlist this partnership, God provided this partnership in Jethro to advise Moses for his success. Some partnerships ordained by blood and God organically create others. Jesus chose the disciples, and the disciples didn't choose one another, yet a partnership was established for them to be "fishers of men" and eventually spread the good news of the gospel.

STEPS OF FAITH

- What partnerships has God organically placed in your midst to give you sound wisdom or assist you with your assignment? List them.

I remember praying to God to provide me mentors to help me toward this calling he placed on my heart, and, without realizing it, He already embedded them into my life. Partnerships were already established before I knew I would one day need their wisdom, guidance, and prayers. As you ask God for partnerships, ask Him to reveal the ones that are already in your midst because He placed them there for you.

Enlisting people on the journey is a lesson I've had to remind myself repeatedly. I know reaching out for help is the wise thing to do, but I don't want to burden or bother people for some reason. Once I removed those foolish thoughts from my head and reached out for help, the people I asked were always gracious and happy to help and offer their expertise. Generally, people like to be a part of something great; in fact, they're thankful and honored to be asked to be part of the journey.

Beyond Jethro's wisdom in spotting Moses' blind spot, he established a blueprint for leaders to establish their team, which we can apply, if necessary, to the mission that God has called you to. Here a few things that stood out to me as valuable tools we can apply:

- Understand you can't do anything alone nor do you want to. According to scripture, God says apart from Him, we cannot do anything.
- We aren't designed to do it alone. It's good and wise to enlist help.
- Be willing to accept advice from wise counsel and remain coachable.
- Never forget that God is always with you. His desire and plan for you is always for your success.
- Be prepared to lead and equip those who are depending on your leadership. Ensure they know what to do and not to do, so there's no confusion and you set them up for success.
- When establishing your team, have a clear understanding of what's needed, so you can find the right person who will fit the need.
- Make sure you seek individuals with honorable character who share your sensibilities.
- Empower your partner or team to move on your behalf. A person or team that knows you have confidence in their abilities can soar.
- Establish a procedure and process, so everyone knows there's a system in place for everything that one would encounter.

Implementing the blueprint above should allow you to create and plan more freely with ease when you share the burden and trust your partnerships. Jethro ends by leaving Moses with this bit of encouragement. "If you do this, God will direct you, you will be able to endure, and all this people also will go to their place in peace." I hope that offers you encouragement and tools in which to soar.

STEPS OF FAITH

- Do you find it hard to reach out for help? Are you reluctant to ask for help? If so, reflect and ponder where this mindset may have originated and process what may be faulty about this mindset. Once you understand its roots that were created to protect you, create and establish a new root of thought that tells you it's in your best interest and ultimate success to endure the edification of others. There's nothing worse than burnout because you tried to do everything by yourself.
- Now I want you to look at the milestones you wrote earlier and see when it will become necessary to enlist outside help? Can you reach out to family or friends? Or will you need to hire a professional business? Before you reach out to professional help, make sure you have exhausted your private network first. Trust me; they'll be honored.
- As I encourage you to seek family and friends' assistance, use good judgment. Not all members

should play a significant role in the assignment God has purposed for your life. Maybe their best contribution is to be a sounding board of encouragement, and that's it. This is where wisdom will be necessary to preserve our precious relationships.

Seek and Receive the Blessing of Partnership

God values partnerships! We see the very first partnership between the Triune God in Genesis 1: 1-3 and verses 26-27. We see this seamless, effortless cooperation between the Godheads that you can, at first glance, miss. The Triune God are fully present in partnership at creation. They're one! God creates Adam to partner with Him to hold dominion over all that He has created. This is humankind's first partnership with our Triune God. This relationship will be our most important partnership that we can have full confidence that this partnership is worthy of trust. Trust is so important in a relationship. Once trust is broken, it may be hard to regain that again. Later, we'll see how the lack of trust Adam and Eve had for God caused their partnership and relationship to be severed. God mentions that it's not good for man to be alone and provides a comparable partnership for Adam in Eve. They're different yet suitable for partnership. Then we see Jesus assemble a team of disciples that would carry on the gospel unbeknownst to them. We see countless biblical accounts of God partnering with His creation to bring about His master plan. What an honor to be given a mandate to partner with Him. And Jesus leaves to ALL who believe in Him the partnership of the Holy Spirit, the Comforter to be with us always. As mentioned in previous chapters, if you don't have a relationship with the Holy Spirit, I implore you to seek the presence of the Holy Spirit to guide, teach, give discernment, direct you in what to say, give you physical power when you need it, and so much more.

In Exodus, we see another beautiful picture of partnership between Moses and Jethro. In Chapter 4:18, we see that Moses requested permission from Jethro, his father-in-law, to return to Egypt to see whether his brothers are still alive, wherefore Jethro gives his blessing to do so. Moses leaves for Egypt with his wife and sons, but, at some point in his mission to lead his people out of Egypt, his family returned to Midian to remain with Jethro because we see Jethro meet Moses in the desert. This beautiful picture of partnership is revealed that's rooted in love, trust, and sacrifice. Jethro assumes the role of head of household in Moses' absence. Jethro provides care and provision for Moses' family while he's on mission.

Now Jethro, Moses' father-in-law, had taken Zipporah, Moses' wife, after he had sent her home, along with her

PART X

two sons. The name of the one was Gershom (for he said, "I have been a sojourner in a foreign land"), and the name of the other, Eliezer (for he said, "The God of my father was my help, and delivered me from the sword of Pharaoh"). Jethro, Moses' father-in-law, came with his sons and his wife to Moses in the wilderness where he was encamped at the mountain of God. And when he sent word to Moses, "I, your father-in-law Jethro, am coming to you with your wife and her two sons with her," Moses went out to meet his father-in-law and bowed down and kissed him. And they asked each other of their welfare and went into the tent. Then Moses told his father-in-law all that the Lord had done to Pharaoh and to the Egyptians for Israel's sake, all the hardship that had come upon them in the way, and how the Lord had delivered them. And Jethro rejoiced for all the good that the Lord had done to Israel, in that he had delivered them out of the hand of the Egyptians.

(Exodus 18:2-9)

Often, we focus on Moses and other well-known individuals, but less known individuals can be lost from the big picture. Jethro can be lost in his contribution to the journey of the Israelites to the Promised Land. Jethro's contribution allowed Moses to focus on the mission at hand without worrying about the welfare of his family. How could Moses successfully lead the Israelites out of Egypt and still lead his family excellently. I want you men and women who feel pressured to be superwomen or supermen to release that burden and know you weren't created to do all of it alone. It took me a long time to understand that it's okay if I don't do it perfectly and ask for help. It doesn't mean that I'm not still striving for excellence, but perfection can leave you riddled with anxieties.

Martin Luther King Jr. and Coretta Scott King come to mind as a partnership that allowed Martin Luther King Jr. to be the great man that he was. Martin had an obligation to his wife and kids along with this great assignment. The only way he could have maintained the cohesiveness of his family was with the agreement and cooperation of his wife Coretta. Coretta's contribution provided stability and a firm foundation from which Martin could travel and lead a significant movement that changed American history forever.

STEPS OF FAITH

- As you look at the mission that God has placed on your heart, whom will you need to enlist?
- Who do you need to be in agreement with and receive their full cooperation in order to move forward in your mission? Is it your spouse, a

family member, or friend? As we pursue the purpose that God has laid on our hearts, we want to make sure we don't shirk our responsibilities at home. We want to make wise decisions that will honor God. God doesn't want us to abandon our responsibilities to our family at the expense of His mission because our loved ones are part of our mission too.

Equally Yoked

The term "equally yoked" is a term mentioned in the bible. If this is a new term to you, it simply is a farming reference when a yoke is placed around the neck of two oxen to ensure they would move forward in the same direction; otherwise, they would go in separate directions. We don't want that, unless that's the intent. When I first read the Bible, I remember not understanding why God told His people not to mingle or marry certain people groups. I thought to myself, That's mean. How can a loving God demand a form of segregation? Why did he encourage the Israelites not to comingle with the other people groups around them? I soon realized it wasn't that He was opposed to them interacting or the people per se, but rather their belief systems.

You shall not intermarry with them, giving your daughters to their sons or taking their daughters for your sons, for they would turn away your sons from following me, to serve other gods. Then the anger of the Lord would be kindled against you, and he would destroy you quickly.

(Deuteronomy 7: 3-4 ESV)

His admonition at its roots was for their protection and success. He knew that the potential for them to get swayed to these other belief systems would ultimately lead them to their demise. They were immersed in the Egyptian culture far longer than they have been in a relationship with God, and He was right. Go to the books of 1st and 2nd Samuel, 1st and 2nd Kings, and 1st and 2nd Chronicles, which document how other influences and the worship of other false gods led them away from obedience to God and ultimately to their captivity. The account of Samson and Delilah deserves observation. In Judges Chapter 13-16, we witness the anointing and tragic fall of Samson. Samson's mother received a visitation from the angel of the Lord announcing she will bear a son after being barren. The child in her womb has been chosen to be a "Nazirite to God in the womb, and he shall begin to save Israel from the hand of the Philistines" (Judges 13: 5 ESV). Prior to this visitation, God allowed the Israelites to be taken captive into the hands of the Philistines for forty years because they did what was evil in God's sight. Here is a partnership that should never have happened. Prayerfully consider your partnerships. Pray who eventually will make up your team. In fact, you should always be praying each step of your journey in realizing your purpose. I also want to mention not all partnerships should require a person to be of the same belief system. If I'm looking for a good plumber, I'm not necessarily looking for a Christian. I want my plumber to be an excellent plumber who can handle the job. Of course, the expectation is that the plumber will do business with integrity and honor despite their faith. However, a long-term partnership should require similar sensibilities to create a cohesive and thriving collaboration. Ultimately, you want a symbiotic relationship. The relationship between the Triune God is harmoniously separate but one. Each person of the Godhead supports the other and is in complete agreement with others; none of the three persons of God contradicts another. That's what we're aiming for in our future partnerships. Nothing is more wearisome than having disagreement and dissension. We want cohesiveness, and establishing the blueprint above should assist with this outcome.

Keep in mind this isn't a sprint. This is a marathon. You want to pace yourself so you can sustain yourself for the journey ahead; you won't experience burnout and abandon the mission by throwing in the towel in defeat. Remember, at award ceremonies, the recipient gets the opportunity to thank everyone who had a stake in their success. All the people who will help you are part of God's master plan and are blessed to be part of the journey.

You're made with purpose for a purpose!

LEGACY:

But lay up for yourselves treasures in heaven, where neither moth nor rust destroys and where thieves do not break in and steal. For where your treasure is, there your heart will be also.

Matthew 6:20-21 ESV

THE REWARD OF FINISHING WELL

Ambassador's Daily Impact

When you hear the word "legacy," what comes to mind? Does it mean leaving a financial inheritance for your offspring? Maybe your goal is to be memorialized somehow, for instance, your name or likeness as a contribution to society. "There's a part in all of us that wants to be remembered, to leave a mark that says I was here, I matter. There's nothing wrong with being remembered fondly. I hope that upon my last breath, when my loved ones lay my physical body to rest, they'll have favorable things to say about my character, my love for them, but, most of all, my desire for them to know the God whose radical love sent His only son Jesus to be their sacrificial lamb. To me, that's a legacy that has lasting power. However, a legacy is not one you can always curate for yourself. Well-known figures like Moses or Martin Luther King, Jr. perceived legacy wasn't one they could manufacture, foresee, or comprehend the fullness of their impact long after they would leave this earth. Oprah Winfrey mentioned in an interview that she built a school for girls in Africa to serve as her legacy, and her mentor, Maya Angelou, said to her, 'You have no idea what your legacy would be because your legacy is every life you've touched. It's every story you've ever told, everybody who heard that story and was affected by that story. It's every person you ever spoke to with a kind word or negative word. Your legacy is every life you've touched.' The intent of the legacy can benefit the one leaving it, or it can be for the benefit of those who will receive it. Let's examine the intent of our legacy. Is the intent to elevate and benefit ourselves? Or is it for the elevation of those who will receive the fruit of our obedience?

Legacy is derived from the Latin word legatus. Its original meaning was "ambassador" or "delegated person." At some point, the word "legacy" seemed to morph into money, material things, and inanimate objects left as an inheritance. However, for the purposes of this chapter, we're going to explore and discover our legacy as an ambassador, a delegated person. We're the legatus, the ambassador, the delegated person selected to be the representative for change. When an ambassador travels to foreign lands, they represent the interests of the country in which they represent. That person is the highest rank sent in place of the president or leader. The mere presence of the Ambassadors changes the atmosphere. From this stance, we will approach the term "legacy." As representatives, what have we been charged with by the One who sent us? How can our presence change the atmosphere?

We impact lives daily positively or negatively. We leave a piece of ourselves whether we realize it or not through a smile, a compliment, a much-needed encouragement, or the generosity of our resources given to us by God. And on the other side of the spectrum, we can also have a negative impact, whether in the form of a scowl, hateful words, ill will, or withholding love, mercy, forgiveness, and kindness. In doing so, we leave a person at a deficit. According to scripture, the power of life and death is in the tongue. What we choose to say or do has the power to give life or destroy. An example of this can be seen in the Book of Job. Job, once a wealthy man revered as a righteous man by all who knew him, including God, receives devastating news after another. He loses his wealth and children, and in the depths of his despair, he experiences excruciating pain in his body that causes him to desire death over life. We learn that his misfortune is no fault of his own, but rather a test allowed by God provoked by Satan to demonstrate his faithfulness to God. What!?

A troubling story, I know. Ultimately, the story ends with Job passing the test and restoring it a hundredfold. However, that's not where I want our focus to remain. In between Job's loss and restoration, he had friends who held power to impact Job positively in the midst of his misery. They held the power of life and death in their tongues yet chose to attack his character and impose blame on him for his misfortune. As we reflect and pursue our greater impact for the Kingdom, let's not minimize our daily impact with those within our family and community whom we interact with intentionally appointed by God. This journey you've elected to take toward clarity of purpose demonstrates your desire to partner with God to give life; to impact lives for the benefit of others and the glory of God. So let it be!

STEPS OF FAITH

- How have you defined legacy for yourself? How do you define it for yourself now?
- Have you ever seen yourself as an ambassador for God? How does that make you feel?
- Now that you're aware of your true legacy, what is the Holy Spirit compelling you to do with this new information?

Your Labor is Not in Vain

"And let us not grow weary of doing good, for in due season we will reap if we do not give up."

Galatians 6:9

PART XI

My favorite fruit is avocado. I love it so much, so I considered planting one. My heart's desire is to one day be able to grab an avocado off my tree whenever the craving arises. However, as I learned what's required to grow avocados and how long it takes for an avocado to bear fruit, I quickly became disheartened. Avocados will not produce avocados in the following season or even the next. It will take years. It could take 5 to 15 years before I get to enjoy the fruit of my labor. My kids would have a greater chance of enjoying them far longer than I would. This information left me uninspired to plant one. If you put time and effort into something, knowing that you won't experience the fruit of your efforts, how would that make you feel? I'm sure that doesn't sound appealing. Who wants to put in all that work and not reap the rewards of their labor? When we put in a day's work, we expect to receive compensation, as we should. The Western culture is steeped in this concept that there has to be something in it for me in order for it to pique my interest or be worthy of my time and effort. I don't want to devalue the wisdom in using your time well or laboring with a reward in mind. However, I want to invite you to consider the possibility that what you were purposed to do may not come with a direct reward to you. Are you okay with that? Is it enough to do it purely out of obedience?

The Bible is filled with many people whose purpose didn't benefit them. In fact, it often came at a deficit, a sacrifice. Moses' purpose of leading the Israelites out of Egypt came at a great cost to him and minimal benefit in the earthly realm other than obedience to the will of his Creator. The same could be said of Joseph and Esther. Joseph, as Egypt's number two in command, had all he needed. He would have been fine during the famine. He didn't have to inconvenience his life, yet he knew it wasn't about him. The God he knows intimately wouldn't allow him to take a posture that we can often take, which is an unwillingness to be inconvenienced without reward. Esther is another example; her life wasn't in danger. She could have remained under the radar, living in the palace, enjoying the good favor she encountered wherever she went. However, the God she knew so intimately wouldn't allow her to dismiss the purpose she was called to accomplish that could very well put her life in danger. With no reward in sight, she risked her comfort and her life to impact the lives of Jewish people. Her selfless act was instrumental in saving a people group from annihilation. While I would have loved to plant an avocado seed today and see the fruit tomorrow, I've come to embrace the fact that the planting of seeds sometimes isn't for you to reap or enjoy but for someone else to reap the benefits.

Moses' purpose of leading the Israelites out of Egypt into the promised land of milk and honey would become his legacy, but for the Israelites, their inheritance. Leading the Israelites to the promised land would be one he would not get to enjoy. He was only given the ability to see it from a distance. I always viewed that moment as God's kindness.

Martin Luther King, Jr. would lead a movement that would change a nation and many generations to come toward greater equality than one he experienced. He wouldn't fully see or experience the fruit of his labor for himself. His labor and sacrifice would be enjoyed by his wife, Coretta, his children, and many beneficiaries, like myself, whom he would never know or meet. For that, I will always be forever thankful for his courage, character, and obedience to his purpose given to him by God. His movement was very much a God movement. His ministry spilled outside the church walls and infiltrated every mountain, valley, suburb, and city of America. Did he start in the civil rights movement, hoping that one day a holiday would be named after him commemorating his contribution to America? I think not! His sole focus was on the mission. His hope was that daily lives would be impacted in such a way that his Black brothers and sisters would not live in fear but experience the fullness of their God-given right to live free from fear. Freedom! As a result, our White brothers and sisters also have the opportunity to benefit from the sin of their forefathers that threatens to entangle to healing and restoration, experiencing more of our Creator's plan for community and His children.

Moses, Joseph, Esther, and Martin Luther King Jr. were Ambassadors, chosen delegates with a mission to complete, and their obedience changed the atmosphere. It changed the course of history, and we are beneficiaries of their obedience.

STEPS OF FAITH

- Do you need to adjust your thinking about what your legacy should look like? Are you willing to keep your eyes on the mission and not the outcome?
- How does it make you feel that you may not receive an earthly reward for your obedience?
- Can you recall a moment when you were thrust into a moment that called for courage and boldness? How did you feel? Were you annoyed, reluctant, or compelled to meet the moment head-on?
- Depending on your answer to the questions above, talk to God about your initial reaction. Ask God to grow in you what you need for future opportunities to be obedient, bold, and courageous.
- As an ambassador, what have you been charged to do with God?

PART XI

Positioned for Purpose, Met with Courage

In the previous chapters, we've sought to clarify our purpose and courage to move toward more of what we were made for. Hopefully, it has become clearer than when you started this journey. I pray God has solidified it for you and sealed it in your heart. While we've gained greater clarity, let's remain open to those unexpected moments that aren't connected to any action steps we can set in motion to reach a goal, but rather remain open to pivotal moments divinely appointed for us to step out on faith and demonstrate courage. Your legacy may very well be one that you didn't set out to accomplish, but you find yourself presented with that call to courage and boldness that changes the trajectory of your life and the lives of everyone around you.

In the Book of Esther, Esther, an orphan raised by Mordecai, her uncle, would be thrust into a defining moment not only for herself and her uncle but for the Jewish people at large. She would be presented with an unexpected moment to exercise boldness and courage. A series of events landed her in the palace in the presence of the king, but, more important than that, she found favor with everyone she encountered, including the king. The favor given to her gave her the unique privilege to have the king's ear that would serve useful when the Jewish people would come to face impending annihilation. She was placed in a position where she could choose to remain silent and safe, unconcerned with the plight of her Jewish brothers and sisters, or meet the moment with boldness and courage. Thankfully, she used her favor from God and position of influence that was not solely for the betterment of her life but rather for the rescue and survival of an entire people group. Thankfully, for the Jewish people, she met the moment with boldness and courage. She approached the king with wisdom and utilized her influence and favor to benefit the Jewish people. She took a risk! Living beyond yourself will always cost something.

Joseph, Jacob's son, is another example of being positioned with purpose. He, too, experienced a series of mishaps that eventually led him to be elevated in a position of great influence. A Hebrew/Israelite by birth, he was chosen to be Pharoah's number two in command. Like Esther, he too was presented with a significant moment that would require him to use the God-given favor bestowed upon him to rescue the Jewish people from starvation. The respect and influence he earned from the Egyptian people placed him in a unique position to advocate for them on their behalf. On their own, the Israelites wouldn't have been able to sway the Egyptians to their plight, but with Joseph's influence, their safety and rescue were secured.

The famous Chesley "Scully" Sullenberger, the pilot who landed the plane on the Hudson River, didn't set out to make that his legacy, yet it will be remembered by many, including those who survived what could have been a catastrophic event. All who witnessed and heard this heroic and successful act would remember it for many years to come. He met this unexpected moment with boldness and courage. His life and the lives of everyone on that plane depended on it. The risk he took paid big dividends. The lives of all the passengers were spared. So, I encourage you to remain bold and courageous to what's in front of you. Lives may depend on your boldness and courage. View the unexpected opportunities you find yourself in as divine positioning so God can do miraculous things through you, thereby giving you a testimony to share His goodness.

STEPS OF FAITH

- Like Esther, where has God placed you in a position of influence that's not solely for your benefit but to benefit a person or group that is disenfranchised in some way?
- Where are you being called to be the voice for the voiceless like Esther, Moses, and Martin Luther King Jr.?
- What will it cost you to use your influence for the betterment of others?
- Like Esther and Scully, they chose to take a risk that paid off. Where might God have placed you to take a risk?

- Who are these disenfranchised people God is laying on your heart? What do you know about them?
- What do you need to do to educate yourself about their obstacles? What does this disenfranchised person or group need? What is their plight?
- How will this disenfranchised person or group benefit from your bold courage?

Pass the Baton

I am fascinated by the Olympics. Athletes from all over the world come to compete, and they have sacrificed and disciplined themselves far beyond what most will ever do. They train for countless hours, days, months, and years for a small window of time that occurs every four years. As I watched the US Women's Relay team prepare to run a race where there are no do-overs, a lot was at stake. The objective is to pass the baton with great precision between the person passing the baton to the one who must ultimately receive it to carry on to the finish line. Their months and years of preparation prepared them for this pivotal moment in time to be empowered to run the Women's Relay to a victorious finish.

I can't help being drawn to Paul's countless references of running the race set before him. Jesus' blood-soaked body hung on the cross, and with His last breath, He uttered, "It is Finished!" What did He finish? He finished the assignment prophesied long before Mary, His mother, was visited by the angel bearing the good news that she would bear a son. The fulfillment of Jesus' life on earth, fully God and fully man, culminated in this transformative moment, a moment of great importance that changes the lives of all who accept His sacrifice on the cross. Bearing the sin and iniquities of humanity, He reconciled our relationship with God forevermore. No more need for an imperfect substitute or mediator. Our 21st-century mindset can cause us to lose the magnitude of this good news and gift because we never had to experience the painstaking process necessary to offer an unblemished lamb as a sacrifice. We never experienced the inability to enter into the Holy of Holies beholden by another to mediate on our behalf. We've been freed from the sacrificial ritual that was expected from His people long ago. We can now go to God anytime and anywhere, no longer separated from our Creator by our sin.

It grieves my heart when the young generation of African Americans are indifferent to the price that has been paid so that they can now experience the freedom that was withheld from their ancestors. The blood sacrificed and shed requires an acknowledgment; it requires a response. A response of gratitude and responsibility. What should that responsibility look like? The responsibility should reflect an understanding of the gift, the sacrifice rendered. Jesus' sacrifice on the cross had long-lasting repercussions that will be felt by many generations to come. We now have direct access to the Creator of all things. We simply need to acknowledge the things that threaten to separate us from God, turn away from what seeks to separate us and turn toward God. It's almost too simple that we neglect to do it or are unwilling to do it, aside from accepting in gratitude the sacrifice made on our behalf. The gratitude should also move us to action, not that the sacrifice is dependent on us to act. Our action is merely a response to what we've been given that we're compelled to share and move on His behalf.

Jesus' expression, "It is finished," is from the Hebrew *tetelestai*, meaning the sacrifice is accomplished, the work is complete, or the debt is paid in full, a term used by the Jewish people after sacrificing animals as a sin offering was complete. However, this time, Jesus, the lamb of God, would finish forevermore what could never be accomplished by the blood of an animal. It was so powerful that it caused the earth to shake; it caused the four-inch thick veil that separated us from the presence of God to be torn from top to bottom. All of creation reverberated in response to what Jesus accomplished on the cross and the finality of what was finished. This baton moving statement, "It is finished," set in motion an invitation to the disciples of that day and us today to continue to carry the baton forward to the finish line. The disciples and followers of that day had no idea what they were about to receive when Jesus told them not to leave Jerusalem. He would give them a life-changing baton, something they would all need to carry on His mission to spread the "good news" to the world. Today, we're given that same baton to carry on the mission until Jesus returns again to fulfill the final prophecy of conquering king. What is this mysterious baton I am alluding to? The one He promised to leave them, the Comforter, the Holy Spirit to carry forward. In every great race, a preparation is required and tools are needed. They were being prepared along the way, and we've been given the same gift today and purpose. Unbeknownst to them and us is that we've been set on this race from the moment we took our first breath to the day we take our last breath. We've been given the baton to receive now, and we're also obligated to give what we've received until the race is done.

STEPS OF FAITH

- We can get desensitized to the magnitude of what was finished on the cross. Take a moment and remember and sit with the fullness of what was finished on your behalf.

- Have you accepted the gift of the Holy Spirit? If not, accept it now. You'll need the power of the Holy Spirit to make it to the finish line.
- Do you feel a sense of responsibility to pass the baton?
- Who have you passed the baton to? And who still needs to receive the baton from you? Make a list and ask God to bring them to mind.

Withholding Nothing in Courage

The song, *Withholding Nothing* by William McDowell embodies Paul, the author of much of the New Testament's posture toward his assignment.

> *I surrender all to you*
> *Everything I give to you*
> *Withholding nothing*
> *Withholding nothing*

Have you ever surrendered yourself to something wholeheartedly? What does it look like to withhold nothing? Could you imagine carving a niche for yourself for years and then being asked to give it up? Or maybe a thought process that you built your whole life as true and have come to realize you were misinformed. That's what Paul, formerly known as Saul of Tarsus, found himself faced with. Sometimes, when something is brought to our attention to change, it may take courage to course-correct, and it won't be easy. It wasn't easy for Paul, and it won't be for you. He was the persecutor of Christians but would later become the most zealous defender and teacher of Christians. He was the least likely person to be chosen to carry on the ministry of Jesus until God redirected him toward his true purpose. He had to surrender his own beliefs to receive the life-changing truth, and it came with a price.

I have prayed that God would grow in me the courage and boldness that Paul exemplified. His life was constantly in jeopardy, but he didn't let that deter him from doing what he was called to do at the moment. He experienced a transformation that he couldn't keep to himself. He was compelled to share it wherever he went, even to the detriment of his life. Paul's clarity and commitment to his assignment reminded me of little Jesus when He was separated from his family after the Festival of the Passover. When His parents realized that the young 12-year-old Jesus was no longer with them, they frantically looked for him. When Jesus was finally found in the Temple by His parents, he met their concern and question with, "Didn't you know I would be at my Father's house?" There was no sarcasm in His question; it was a matter of fact. He was saying, "You should have known this is where I would be because it's for this purpose I have come." He was clear on His purpose and surrendered to it, withholding nothing.

Our job is to surrender wholeheartedly, withholding nothing! If Paul were alive today, he would have most certainly racked up many frequent flyer miles if flying were an option for him. He was a man on a mission! Paul is known for his missionary journeys to spread the gospel. He traveled by foot and boat and often not in the best of accommodations. No matter the route, circumstance, or mode of travel, he never was in doubt, confused, or swayed from his purpose. He understood the urgency of his assignment. Paul tends to make references to running a race and finishing well. He wanted to finish the race he had been given without any regrets.

> *However, I consider my life worth nothing to me: my only aim is to finish the race and complete the task the Lord Jesus has given me—the task of testifying to the good news of God's grace.*
>
> Acts 20:24 (NIV)

We can often get on this hamster wheel of life, exerting so much energy that we can have this false impression that we're accomplishing a lot, but not really. Or we put forth a lot of energy toward the things that pull us away from what we were put on this earth to accomplish. We put our energy into the things that bear fruit, but is it the right fruit? Is it long-lasting? Paul realizes that his life is worth nothing if he doesn't finish the assignment given to him by God, his true purpose. Prior to his life-changing encounter with Jesus, which transformed the trajectory of his life, he was convinced his assignment's purpose was to purge his society of the scourge that he thought were the Christians. He was busy doing what he thought was his purpose with urgency and passion until God revealed to him his purpose was not to destroy the Christians but, rather, to impart to them the transformational power of Jesus because he experienced it.

He was no longer confused about his true purpose. He says, with such clarity that he was "given the task of testifying to the good news of God's grace." What does it look like for you to testify to the good news of God's grace? Is it teaching, preaching, or acknowledging the plight of those powerless to advocate for themselves like the orphans, seniors, sick, mentally impaired, immigrants, persecuted, poor, forgotten, or abused? Do you see advocating for the disenfranchised as testifying to the good news of God's grace? Whatever God has given you a heart for, it was placed there by God. I encourage you to pursue it zealously as Paul did with the task that was given to him to complete. God enlarged Paul's capacity to love rather than hate the Christians he once held with such disdain. He is now moved with such great compassion and responsibility to those who need God's grace, and it didn't just end with the Gentiles. He also held that for those he once directed to destroy: the Christians.

STEPS OF FAITH

- What part of your life are you withholding from God? Once you've identified what it is, courageously trust Him with it.
- Who is God enlarging your heart's capacity to love?
- As Paul was redirected, ask God to reveal to you where you may need redirection in your understanding of Him or your true purpose?

Fulfillment of Purpose

Let's shift our focus and concern from the earthly understanding of legacy to finishing well what we were purposed to complete, which is the true legacy we should pursue. *Therefore, I declare to you today that I am innocent of the blood of any of you. For I have not hesitated to proclaim to you the whole will of God. Acts 20: 26 (NIV)* Have you ever experienced the feeling of having no regrets because you have given your whole self to something of great value to you? How did it feel? Paul describes his sense of peace once he was redirected and the fulfillment of knowing he has no regrets. His conscience is clear. He knows he has done what was expected of him by his Creator; if anyone reaped the consequences of their action, it wasn't a result of him not warning them, not doing what he was purposed to do. Their demise would not be something he would bear the responsibility for.

What do you think about Paul declaring that he is innocent of their blood? Is he right in thinking he bears some responsibility toward those God has placed in His sphere of influence? As a recovering codependent, I am super sensitive to bearing responsibility for the actions of others. I've become vigilant in ensuring that I'm not taking the role of savior because there's only One who saves, and it's not me. However, unlike Paul, Jonah's initial unwillingness to warn the people of Nineveh wasn't met with the realization that he would bear some culpability if God destroyed the Ninevites. But God is ever so patient with us. He dealt with Jonah's heart that enabled him to enlarge his heart to the Ninevites' disposition. God is always inviting us to enlarge our capacity to love rather than hate. In our ability to love, we testify to the good news of God's grace.

God invites us to pray for our enemies. Praying for our enemies is a concept that seems foolish and weak to the world, but God's ways are never our ways. His thoughts are not like our thoughts. God says the world will know we are His children by the way we love. Jesus, nearly at the end of Himself, utters to His Father in Heaven, "Forgive them Father for they know not what they do." This capacity of love doesn't come easily to us. I know it doesn't come easily to me apart from His goodness. On my own, I'm prone to dismiss, discount, distance myself, and, I admit, avenge myself. What Jesus models is always contrary to our instinctive behavior and construct of this world.

STEPS OF FAITH

- Paul seems to demonstrate his awareness of his purpose. He acknowledges he bears no responsibility because he completed what was his to do. Do you agree that Jonah would have shared some culpability for the destruction of the Ninevites had he not delivered his warning? If not, why?
- When were you like Paul prior to his conversion of persecuting the Christians or Jonah when he refused to warn the Ninevites? Ask God for his grace and forgiveness. Our God is extremely generous to forgive and extend mercy to a repentant and obedient heart. Let his grace and love for you envelop you. How does it feel to experience this love and grace? Bask in it!
- How is God inviting you or challenging you to enlarge your capacity to love?
- Do you accept this challenge to share the good news of God's grace in the way He has uniquely created you for?

PART XI

Pursuing the Crown

We tend to pursue accolades that are great for the moment but forgotten after time. We work hard for trophies made of metal and certificates made of paper that can be destroyed. Don't misunderstand me! I love recognition, and being affirmed by my peers in my field is nice, especially if your love language is affirmation or gifts. Who doesn't want to be acknowledged or rewarded to indicate the mastery of their field of choice? We reward our kids for a job well done to encourage them to continue. Whatever you do, do it in the name of the Lord. However, if we're honest with ourselves, our work has the potential to be unto ourselves and for our glory alone. As an actress, the mere construct of the entertainment industry is, at its core, self-promotion, and everyone is catering to the narrative that it's all about you, a slippery slope that can cause one to be a casualty if not careful. I can easily pursue the reward given in the earthly realm that is temporal and lose sight of the reward awaiting me that will be long-lasting. Paul says it best here: *"I have fought a good fight, I have finished my course, I have kept the faith: Henceforth there is laid up for me a crown of righteousness, which the Lord, the righteous judge, shall give me at that day: and not to me only, but unto all them also that love his appearing"* 2 Timothy 4: 7-8 (ESV) We can get consumed and occupied with what it takes to get ahead here on earth and lose sight of the crown that awaits for finishing the race well. And I am not implying that we have to work to get into heaven. God did all that was needed. Our job is to acknowledge and accept what He has done as a gift.

Paul has this unwavering confidence that he has finished the course given to him to run in faith. He understands that there is a crown not made of metal, far more priceless, that will be given by our righteous judge to all God's faithful servants. Paul used the analogy of running a race, and it's so appropriate for the life he led and the life we've decided to embark on. He ran it with urgency, intentionality, humility, and courage, knowing he had done all that he was given to do. May you embody this same confidence as you run the race set before you. Your crown of righteousness is waiting for you. Ambassador, Go Forth!

You're made with purpose for a purpose!

VISIT FOR RESOURCES AND UPDATES AT

www.ShirleyCharlesRobinson.com

OTHER WAYS TO CONNECT:

FB Made With Purpose For A Purpose
IG madewithpurpose_forapurpose